The
Kindergarten Wars

The
Kindergarten Wars

THE BATTLE
TO GET INTO AMERICA'S
BEST PRIVATE SCHOOLS

Alan Eisenstock

WARNER BOOKS

Some of the individuals in the book have asked me to respect their anonymity. Therefore, I have modified their identities and certain details about them.

Warner Books
Hachette Book Group USA
1271 Avenue of the Americas
New York, NY 10020

Visit our Web site at www.HachetteBookGroupUSA.com.

Printed in the United States of America

First Edition: September 2006
10 9 8 7 6 5 4 3 2 1

Warner Books and the "W" logo are trademarks of Time Warner Inc. or an affiliated company. Used under license by Hachette Book Group USA, which is not affiliated with Time Warner Inc.

Library of Congress Cataloging-in-Publication Data

Eisenstock, Alan.
   The kindergarten wars : the battle to get into America's best private schools / Alan Eisenstock.
      p. cm.
   ISBN-13: 978-0-446-57774-8
   ISBN-10: 0-446-57774-X
   1. Private schools—United States—Admission. 2. Kindergarten—United States—Admission. I. Title.
   LC49.E57 2006
   372.21'8—dc22   2006006824

To B. J. K. and Z.
Always

Contents

Kid on Spec

The following story, like all of the stories in this book, is true:

Gracie Graham, fifty-three, director of the prestigious Bright Stars Nursery School, sat in her office with Monica Keane, thirty-one, a prospective parent uniformed in pale Donna Karan and enough Tiffany to open her own store. For the first forty minutes of their visit, Gracie had taken Monica on a tour of the preschool, formerly a cheerless basement in a Methodist church, now a cluster of rooms bathed in soft colors, a mauve, an azure, a tapioca, teeming with thirty darling, exuberant children of many shapes and cultures. Years ago, in the early stages of Bright Stars, Gracie, then a young teacher fresh out of college, helped name these classrooms after insects preceded by inviting adjectives: the Busy Bees, the Giddy Grasshoppers, the Lucky Lightning Bugs.

Today the children were up to their elbows in cake batter, absorbed in a cooking project. Looming over them, cheering them on, lending a hand, were two aging hippie women, quiet talkers, known only by their first names, which coincidentally matched the seasons. Monica could barely contain her excitement, letting slip an involuntary "Ohhh" at the sight of an adorable mop-

haired Busy Bee smearing frosting over the top of a layer cake, her tongue poking out of her mouth in concentration.

Within moments of meeting her, Gracie could tell that Monica was a woman with questions, questions that indicated more than a casual interest in Bright Stars, and judging by the cash value of the jewelry strewn along her left forearm alone, a prospective parent of means. Not that this was a ticket in. Not by a long shot. But it was, let's face it, a good place to start.

Monica had also done her homework. Sitting across from Gracie in her office, she glanced at her BlackBerry and asked, "Would you describe Bright Stars as progressive or academic?"

Academic preschool, Gracie thought. *Talk about an oxymoron. When did it come to this?*

"I'd say we were developmentally appropriate," Gracie said, the words rolling out of her mouth, packaged, as if she were running for political office. "Of course, these days with parents enrolling their kids in *pre*-preschool, drilling their kids with flash cards, trying to force them to read at age two, I'm not sure where we're going anymore."

"I completely agree," Monica said. She pinpricked her Black-Berry. "What's your policy on TV? Do the children watch DVDs in the classroom?"

"Not as a rule. On occasion, for example when it rains, we'll put on *Blue's Clues*, something like that. Or after lunch we might pop in *Winnie the Pooh* while the children are closing their eyes, gearing up for the afternoon."

"I can certainly relate to *that*," Monica said.

The women nodded and smiled. Monica slid her BlackBerry into her purse and leaned forward. It was at that point that they each dropped the pretense and began what could actually be called a conversation. At dinner that night Gracie would relate

to friends that there was even a sense of connection. It seemed real at the time. Honest. True. Then, after spending close to an hour with Monica Keane, a woman who had to be considered a strong Bright Stars candidate, Gracie said, "So, tell me about your child."

"Oh," Monica said, "I don't have a child."

Gracie's smile remained frozen on her face. "Are you . . . pregnant?"

"No," Monica said, "but we're thinking of trying soon."

"Then . . . what are you doing here?" The words trickled out in a stunned monotone.

"It's so hard to get into a top-tier kindergarten in this city. I wanted to get a head start."

"Uh-huh," Gracie said. She realized now that her lips had clamped into a tight thin line. She said nothing more. She assumed, at this point, that Monica would take her silence as a cue, pack up her Prada purse, and leave.

But Monica leaned even farther forward in her chair and said in a whisper, "Gracie, between us, how do we get in?"

Gracie abruptly stood up.

"You can start by having a *kid*," she said.

How Do You Get In?

How do you get in?

Not only is this the question that parents pose endlessly during the process of applying to private school kindergarten, it is the engine that drives the process itself. As the father of two children in private school and a trustee on the school's board of directors, I became fascinated by the question. Once my tenure as a trustee came to an end, I saw that fewer and fewer kindergarten spots were available. A spot in our school's kindergarten had become a coveted prize. I began to realize that getting in and getting an education were vastly different processes. I started to hear stories—funny stories, crazy stories, horror stories—of desperate parents doing anything to gain a space in kindergarten.

As I thought about these stories and read what people were doing to get into private school kindergarten in every city in the country, as well as in Japan, Spain, and other countries, I became even more intrigued. Then I got hooked. I left the board and began researching this book.

Early on I decided to remove my former school from the story. The director of admissions and the head of school remain dear friends. I am indebted to them. I would not have been able to write this book without their guidance. When I got lost, they pointed me in the right direction; when I needed an introduction, they made a call. But they do not appear in the book and the school is not depicted.

Writing and researching *The Kindergarten Wars* consumed more than two years of my life. I followed families who applied to private schools in various cities, including Atlanta, Baltimore, Boston, Chicago, Detroit, Los Angeles, Nashville, New Orleans, New York, San Francisco, and Seattle. With only slight variations, the process itself and the parents' angst that accompanied it were strikingly similar in all of the cities. The exception was New York, which, as in most things, stood out as if in its own orbit. This is partly due to its long tradition of private school education dating back to the formation of the very first private school in the United States, Collegiate, founded in 1628. It's also partly due to the nature of New Yorkers themselves, Manhattanites mostly—prideful, competitive, independent, and insistent on attaining what they perceive to be the best. In addition, applicants to almost all private school kindergartens in New York are required to take the ERB, an IQ-type test administered one-on-one to preschoolers by a professional examiner. Virtually every other private school in the country evaluates prospective kindergartners to some degree, but only the New York private schools require a formal scored and written evaluation as a precondition for entrance.

At the completion of my research, I decided to concentrate on four families, focusing on four moms. I found that in general moms took the lead in the application process. The exceptions were three dads, one in Nashville, one in Boston, and one in Detroit. These dads told me that they took charge of the process for the same two reasons: they knew prominent people at the schools they applied to and they were unabashed game players.

As well as knowing several people whose children attended the school he coveted for his son, the Boston dad is an accomplished amateur photographer. He volunteered to document school assemblies, the All-School Holiday Program, and the fifth grade graduation ceremony, for free.

"I have no doubt that my presence at the school was the reason my son got in," he said.

The other two dads leaned heavily on relationships. The Detroit dad concentrated on one particular school because a college fraternity brother was on the board of directors. His child got in. The Nashville dad was told that getting into private school was "all about letters of recommendation." His friends urged him to submit two strong letters from two very significant people, people his friends helped him solicit.

"The letters were the only factors that made our application stand out," he said. "It was clear I wasn't going to be contributing big money."

It worked. A top-tier private school accepted his daughter.

For the most part, though, it was all about the moms. They scouted the schools, attended the open houses, toured the campuses, and winnowed their choices to the ones that reflected their educational philosophies and lifestyles. They were the ones who filled out the applications (at least the first drafts) and drove their kids to their school visits. The dads often took a backseat, joining their wives for tours of only the most serious contenders and, of course, participating in the parent interview. In some cases, dads emerged from the background to attempt to close the deal.

The four moms I followed represent a cross section of typical soldiers in the kindergarten wars. All four of the moms attended college; two have advanced degrees. Lauren is a stay-at-home mom and a woman of means due to her husband's lucrative business. Trina is a single mom of ethnic diversity, struggling to make a go of her career. Shea is a New York mom who works part-time, her husband providing the bulk of their income.

The fourth mom, Katie, is as close to a "regular" mom as anyone could be. Financially, she and her husband fall solidly into what we once called the middle class. Her husband works long hours and brings home a good salary. Katie has put her career on hold temporarily in order to devote herself to her kids. She entered the private school application process reluctantly, after much research and soul-searching. She admits now that she was naïve, unprepared for the culture shock that rudely slapped her across the face.

All of the moms gave me the gift of total cooperation and generosity. I became their shadow, accompanying them on school visits, open houses, and tours. When it was impossible for me to observe a part of the process firsthand, they would phone me immediately afterward and re-create what they had experienced moments before, down to the dialogue that had been spoken. Katie in particular and perhaps uniquely is a copious note taker, habitually scribbling paragraphs of thoughts, impressions, descriptions, and emotions into the notebook she always carries in her purse. She would willingly describe her moods and emotions, even when they came out in a whirlwind of extremes. Katie pulled no punches. She bared her soul. This book became her de facto diary, her private school confessional.

A final note about my families.

I felt confident that I would have no trouble finding people who would be willing to share the application process with me, as long as they weren't identified by name. I was wrong. Although many parents were intrigued by the prospect of appearing in a book on this subject, more than a dozen turned me down. Most offered apologies. One mom provided an explanation:

"I don't want anyone to know where I didn't get in. Or, God forbid, that I didn't get in at all."

•   •   •

My goal in *The Kindergarten Wars* is to show all sides of the application process. In addition to following parents, I was determined to follow admissions directors and school heads to see what the process was like from their perspective. From my previous experience and from what friends in the "business" told me, I assumed I would experience dozens of doors slammed in my face.

To my great surprise, many admissions directors and school heads were eager to speak to me. They were open, frank, and generous with their time. Several allowed me access to their inner sanctums, offering me glimpses into the nuts and bolts of their admissions process, access that I doubt had ever before been granted to an outsider. It was as if I had offered them the opportunity to set the record straight. I was pleased to give them a forum to express themselves and to show prospective parents for the first time what really goes on behind the scenes.

Some school officials refused to talk to me. Others agreed to be interviewed but managed to avoid saying anything substantial in the course of our hour together. They suddenly became a version of a presidential press secretary glibly appearing to answer questions when in fact they were dodging and weaving, ducking behind evasive language or deftly veering off the subject. If I persisted, they employed more direct tactics. When I asked one admissions director, "Why did you choose this particular child?" she stopped taking my calls. Previously, she had been my most forthcoming and available school contact. Now she had ceased to exist, as if she'd been swept away into a witness protection program.

The most dramatic and bizarre moment of my research occurred one cold and rainy morning when I interviewed the director of a preschool. When the interview began, I sensed reluctance, even regret that she had agreed to see me. I dismissed this, chalking it up to the presence of my tape recorder. The interview proceeded smoothly, pleasantly, until I asked this question:

"I hear repeatedly that directors of admission rely heavily on their relationships with preschool directors. Is that true?"

"Turn the tape recorder off right now," the preschool director said.

"I'm sorry?"

"*Now.*"

I was so thrown by the violence of her response that I reflexively reached over and snapped off the recorder. She shifted abruptly in her chair. I thought for certain that she was about to ask me to leave.

In the process of researching five books and countless magazine articles involving thousands of hours of conversations, including interviewing someone with ties to the Mob, nobody had ever asked me to stop the tape recorder. Now I had the distinct feeling that I was about to be kicked out of a *preschool*. Clearly, I had hit a nerve. I knew then that this subject was far more sensitive and explosive than I imagined.

I wanted to erase this blemish on my record. I apologized and promised I would keep my questions more general and less probing. She agreed to finish the interview. I turned the tape recorder back on and we ran through some generic questions about her preschool program. She revealed nothing useful for the book but at least I wasn't tossed out into the rain in front of a dozen finger-painting three-year-olds.

Ultimately, though, other admissions directors and school heads revealed more about the admissions process than I would ever have imagined. There was only one condition. I could not use their names or the names of their schools. One school head requested that I change her gender and move the location of her school to another city to protect her identity.

I not only agreed, I decided ultimately to set the book in an anonymous American city. Except for the sections in New York, *The Kindergarten Wars* might take place in any of a dozen cities across the country from Boston to San Francisco, Dallas to Detroit. Since I discovered that the private school application process is more or less universal, and to protect every person's and every school's identity, the city where the narratives take place is never named.

I have used real names only a few times in the book, such as in the cases of Pastor Sweetie Williams, his son Eliezer, Manasa Tangalin, and Emily Glickman, a New York educational consultant who requested that I use her name. In every other instance, I changed their names, created composites, and invented personality traits. The result is that the schools and people are real but camouflaged by my imagination. What I didn't change were conversations. The dialogue in the following pages comes from tapes I recorded or as a result of conversations I witnessed, heard, or was told about firsthand.

• • •

At its core *The Kindergarten Wars* is the story of a quest. The prize our four families seek is as elusive as a cloud. To complicate matters, they are in competition with scores of other seekers, many accustomed to getting what they want, when they want it, and damn the cost. The term that describes these people is *entitled*—the "E word," one director of admissions calls it. When the powers protecting the prize withhold it from even the entitled, the result is a deep and pervasive societal anxiety, edging to communal frustration, bubbling toward rage. In her novel *Admissions*, Nancy Lieberman calls the private school application process in Manhattan a "blood sport." Taking this image to a Faustian level, Judith Warner in her book *Perfect Madness: Motherhood in the Age of Anxiety* writes, "We are convinced that every decision we make, every detail we control, is *incredibly important*," adding, "Parents prostitute their souls for spots in private schools."

Before I began researching this book, I believed this was an exaggeration and that these parents were exceptions. There are so many choices, I thought, so many schools: charter schools, magnet schools, specialized schools within schools, parochial schools. Indeed, many of the educators I interviewed across the country promoted these and other public school alternatives.

To begin with, though, exclusivity sells. The more exclusive the prize, the more we want it. The head of a relatively low-key private school said to me jokingly, "Just once I want to start out the application process by saying, 'Sorry. We have no spots available at all this year. We are completely full. I am not taking any applications. You cannot get into this school,' just to see what would happen. My theory is that the more exclusive you are the more people want you."

There is no end in sight. The elements of exclusivity and elitism are, if anything, multiplying. Once a child has been admitted into kindergarten, a high likelihood exists that the child's siblings will also be invited in, barring any evidence of high-risk behavior or serious learning differences. The oldest child becomes the pioneer. A mom of three children said, "All the pressure is on my oldest. If he gets in, his brother and sister will get in because they're sibs. In other words, *he'll* get them in."

Beyond siblings having first crack at kindergarten openings (schools generally decide on siblings months ahead of the other applicants), there is also *legacy*, nothing new in Manhattan and in some other cities, but a recent phenomenon that is further breeding exclusivity throughout the country. As "newer" private schools celebrate thirty or more years of existence, the children of their graduates are reaching kindergarten age. These alumni children, legacies, stand with siblings as the recipients of the first available kindergarten spots. Two directors of admissions bemoaned the fact that because of sibs and legacies they had only four kindergarten openings available to the "general public." One school had exactly two openings. Another admissions director admitted that because of legacy, she typically has no openings in kindergarten. With higher numbers of siblings and legacies waiting in the wings, the circle of exclusivity appears unbreakable.

Many of the parents I interviewed considered their local public schools. They went on tours and to open houses. They talked to teachers, principals, and parents who were committed to the concept of public school.

"I did all the research. I really wanted to like my neighborhood school," a mom in San Francisco said to me, "but it wasn't good enough. Why shouldn't I strive for the best for my child? Why should I have to settle for something that I know is less?"

Some parents visited their neighborhood schools and were pleasantly surprised. They found facilities that were in good working order, walls that were freshly painted, several available computers, libraries with fully stocked shelves, and well-equipped science labs and art rooms. The teachers seemed capable, the children engaged and happy. These were decent schools.

The problem is that's the *best* they were. Decent. Acceptable.

And so by choice or necessity, many parents of the new generation of prospective kindergartners begin their quest for a spot in private school. If they succeed, if they are lucky enough to get in, their reward is a top-notch education and a tuition bill that through twelfth grade will amount to $500,000 per child. That's $500,000 *B.C.*

Before College.

Is it worth it?

Truthfully, it's hard to know until our kindergartners grow into taxpaying adults and involved citizens; we may have to wait thirty years for the answer. Perhaps we're seeking the answer to a different question. Given the perceived state of public education and the ever-increasing competition to get into college, is spending $500,000 to educate each child *necessary*?

To many parents, and not all of them card-carrying members of the elite, the answer is a resounding *yes*.

The
Kindergarten Wars

CHAPTER ONE

The $500,000 Question

The Three C's

From the moment the idea for this book inflicted itself on me, before I began meeting with admissions directors and following families around the country, friends, colleagues, and acquaintances who were frantically applying to private school kindergarten began bombarding me with questions: Is private school that much better than public school? Will getting into an elite kindergarten get my kid into an elite college? Do people of diversity have an edge? What should I write on the application to make me stand out? What are admissions directors looking for in the interview? Are there really such things as feeder nursery schools? Do first-choice letters matter? Do siblings automatically get in? Do people buy their way in? Is a private school education worth $500,000 per child from kindergarten through twelfth grade?

This book attempts to answer those questions.

But the first question everyone wanted answered, the one that encompasses most of the others and stands above them all, remains:

How do you get in?

After two years of talking to dozens of admissions directors, school heads, college counselors, educational consultants, teachers, and preschool directors, I can honestly say . . . I don't know. When I posed the question to admissions directors and school heads, I was greeted by bewildered looks, vacant stares, uncomfortable shrugs, and one actual scratch of the head.

"I go by instinct," an admissions director told me.

"The process is not an art," another director of admissions said, "and it's certainly not a science. It's a feeling. At the end of the day, both the school and the parents are taking a leap of faith."

"The decision-making is intuitive," a school head said. "We can reduce it to numbers if you want to. I'm sure that works for a lot of people. I've been doing this for so long that the system I've created over time has become a sort of nonsystem. But it works."

Apparently, I'm not the only one who doesn't know the answer; the people who actually make the decisions don't know either.

Except I don't believe them.

I believe that the admissions directors and school heads of top-tier private schools know exactly what they're doing because they have certain needs and obligations they have to fulfill. They know which siblings, legacies, and children of faculty, diversity, and prominence they're letting in. The "no-brainers," one admissions director called them. I believe that their instincts, intuition, and leaps of faith are reserved for what another director of admissions called the "leftovers," the "regular people," when and if they have openings.

"Every school wants normal folks," an educational consultant told me. "They all want people who are going to bust their butts, work hard, and be present. Otherwise, God forbid, they might be seen as elitist."

. . .

People apply to private school for one or more of three reasons. I call them *the Three C's*: children, college, and country club.

All of the parents I followed applied to private school kindergarten primarily because they felt it was in the best interest of their children, the first *C*. Shea Cohen, who lives on the Upper East Side of Manhattan, said, "For us, it really is about the education. We want the best for our kids. We are not a family with unlimited resources. We will take a serious financial hit paying for private school. But we're willing to do that because education is our number one priority."

Beyond that, Shea said that sending her children to her public school was out of the question. "We want to raise our kids in the city. We're not going to move. The public school that our children would have to go to looks like a prison. And we live in a really nice neighborhood. So we're stuck. Out of options."

Shea was not speaking from an elitist perspective. MK, director of admissions at Longbourne, a prestigious private school in Manhattan, echoed Shea's feelings. "Public schools are not an option. That is not just a perception. There are maybe half a dozen on the grammar school level that I think are decent. That is the sad part of the story. Used to be public schools were better. Not anymore. I hate that that's happening but you cannot deny it. You cannot put your head in the sand."

Ruth, an educational consultant, echoed MK's feelings. "It used to be that everybody just went to their local school. There were smarties, dummies, fatties, skinnies, rich kids, poor kids, and everything was fine and you learned how to live in the world. That's just the way it was."

In another city, Katie Miller, one of the moms I followed, toured her local public school twice. The first time she was disappointed. She went back a second time to be sure.

"I wanted to like it," she said. "Believe me, I tried."

Her neighborhood school was spread out into three long diagonal sections resembling a giant M. The walls were industrial gray and in need of new paint. The library, where she met for a kindergarten "roundup," was a long rectangular room with worn carpeting and dull brown walls. A cluster of iMac computers huddled near the door. They were blue and enormous and eight years out-of-date. The teachers who spoke to the prospective parents were all over forty and well-meaning, but their presentations were uninspired.

"They seemed lovely but they were exhausted, burned to a crisp," Katie said, and paused. "And I have to be honest. Spanish is the first language for over fifty percent of those kids. That's huge. These kids are just learning English and my daughter is *reading*. That concerns me. Will she be pushed aside?"

Lauren Pernice, the third mom I followed, lives in an exclusive neighborhood that, by reputation, is home to one of the top public elementary schools in her city.

"I checked it out," she said. "My first impression was confusion. Lots of traffic. Parking hassles. Cars negotiating with each other. It struck me as very disorganized. I watched for a while, then came home and called a friend who's an educator. She said, look, it really is a good public school. She called it enriching. But she was afraid that it might not be flexible enough for my son. It might not teach to his level."

Lauren decided to visit a kindergarten class. What she saw

made her feel slightly better. The teachers seemed skilled, the children engaged, the facilities decent. It was fine. But Lauren wanted more than *fine* for her child.

"I want a school that offers the academics that Killian needs and is nurturing enough to give him individual attention. Academically, he's quite advanced, but socially I think he could use a little help. He's not going to get that in our public school. There are just too many kids."

Finally, I followed Trina D'Angelo, a single mom, who for safety reasons refused to consider her local school.

"Send my son there? I wouldn't *drive* by there," she said.

• • •

When these same parents visited private schools, their jaws dropped. Objectively speaking, there was no comparison. An educational consultant described it this way: "It's like comparing apples and tuna fish. You are not even in the same category."

The private schools they toured offered state-of-the-art music and art rooms; theaters and science labs that would make actors and scientists drool; libraries rivaling those found on college campuses; sparkling new gymnasiums; cutting-edge technology centers; class sizes that rarely exceeded twenty students, often limited to fifteen; *two* teachers in every classroom, invariably young, dynamic, nurturing, and enthusiastic about what they were teaching because they helped design the curriculum; a bank of computers in every classroom; green, parklike school grounds; open playing fields and intricate redwood play structures; after-school programs offering courses from yoga to knitting to karate; hot lunch choices that were either catered or presented in spotless cafeterias resembling corner coffee shops ("I eat at my kid's school twice a week," a mom said. "The food is terrific"); and kindergartners who would routinely surprise their teachers with impromptu hugs. The touring parents also encountered a sense of community in every school they visited; these schools felt like homes away from home. The kids wanted to be there. And often so did the parents.

•   •   •

According to our current political administration, we have entered "a new era in education," more commonly described by the hopeful yet problematic catchphrase "No Child Left Behind." But in fact, many parents living in or near cities consider the school possibilities available to them and come away with a sad and frustrating conclusion. Their school choices are limited. The public schools, whether the parents' perceptions are factual or apocryphal, are no choice at all. City schools are overcrowded, underfunded, poorly staffed, and seem unsafe. And as the architects of NCLB claim, many are failing. Parents are inundated with reports of this in the media. A *Los Angeles Times* headline screams, "13% of State's Public Schools in Peril of Failure" (October 13, 2004). According to the rules of NCLB, a failing school has three years to "succeed," meaning its students from third through eighth grade must achieve minimum scores on a standardized math and reading test they are given each year. If the students don't pass the test, the school is deemed "failing," funds may be cut off, and the school may be closed.

Parents who fear that the public schools teach to the lowest common denominator see a broken system on the brink of becoming irreparable as teachers, in order to bring up test scores, teach to the lowest-performing children in the class. As educator, author, and editor George Wood writes in the book *Many Children Left Behind: How the No Child Left Behind Act Is Damaging*

Our Children and Our Schools (Beacon Press, 2004), "Many of the supporters of NCLB have good intentions, hoping for schools to work even harder to meet the needs of our children. Unfortunately their intentions have been hijacked by a one-size-fits-all, blame-and-shame agenda that will do nothing to help our schools and will only exacerbate an already unfortunate trend." In the same book, renowned Stanford education professor Linda Darling-Hammond says, simply, "The biggest problem with the NCLB act is that it mistakes measuring schools for fixing them."

Late in 2005, Education Secretary Margaret Spellings acknowledged the flaws inherent in NCLB and attempted to alter the law by proposing that students' success be measured by individual improvement, as opposed to forcing each student to reach a predetermined score. In an editorial entitled "Some States Left Behind" (November 28, 2005), the *Los Angeles Times* credits Spellings for at least attempting to "bring some sanity to a law so unworkable that it was causing even some solidly Republican states to rebel against the Bush administration." The editorial slams NCLB further, stating, "The new rules, though admirable, cannot overcome the limitations of a law that was well-intentioned but ill-conceived, clumsily crafted and drastically under-funded. The major contribution of No Child Left Behind is that it has revealed how badly impoverished students are doing—and how little many schools were doing about it."

Fixing our public school crisis requires vision and the means to finance that vision. Educators working in conjunction with concerned parents and citizens and well-intentioned politicians endlessly debate new ways to revamp or revitalize NCLB. But as of this writing our nation is distracted by the costs of homeland security, a Middle East war, and the aftermaths of Hurricanes

Katrina, Rita, and Wilma. Solutions to our crisis in public education, and the financing of those solutions, will have to wait. However, when it comes to our children, time is the last thing we have.

• • •

On May 17, 2000, the American Civil Liberties Union sued the State of California, claiming that the state deprives tens of thousands of low-income students of the bare necessities to receive a quality education. An article in the *Los Angeles Times*, "Suit on Schools Near Resolution" (July 10, 2004), describes the details of the class-action lawsuit, filed in San Francisco Superior Court on behalf of more than sixty students in eighteen elementary and high schools throughout California. The lawsuit, *Williams v. California*, named after an Oakland middle school student, Eliezer Williams, states that the sixty students were subjected to the following conditions in their schools: "no textbooks, outdated or defaced textbooks; no access to a library; no or not enough basic school supplies; no or not enough labs or lab materials; no or not enough access to computers; no access to music or art classes; no or too few guidance counselors; as few as 13% of teachers with full teaching credentials; chronically unfilled teacher vacancies; heavy reliance on substitute teachers; no homework assignments due to lack of materials; massive overcrowding in the classes, including classes without seats and desks; cramped, makeshift classrooms; multi-track schedules that prevent continuous, year-to-year study in a given subject; multi-track schedules that force students to take key exams before completing the full course of study; broken or nonexistent air conditioning or heating systems, resulting in extremely hot or cold classrooms; toilets that don't flush; toilets that are filthy with urine, excrement, or blood; toilets that are locked; hazardous facilities, including broken windows, walls, and ceilings; leaky roofs and mold; and infestations of rats, mice, and cockroaches." Finally, after more than four years, the state and the ACLU settled out of court for $1 billion, money that will be used to repair 2,400 schools across California over an indeterminate period of time. The article quotes Pastor Sweetie Williams, the father of the plaintiff in the case, as being "thrilled that an agreement had been reached.

"I thank God that it's coming to an end," Williams said. "This has been a great opportunity not only to help my children but also to remind parents that we've got to stand up for what is right."

The state of American public schools, especially in our cities, is truly shameful. Our schools have not failed; we have failed our schools.

· · ·

Pastor Sweetie Williams is in his mid-fifties, a gentle, soft-spoken man. The timbre of his voice exudes kindness. A pastor for over twenty years, he is courteous in the way of many former military men, of whom he is one.

"The lawsuit started when Eliezer was in seventh grade," he says. "He would come home after school and he would never do any homework. I asked him about it and he said that he didn't have any books. I went to the teacher. It was true. There were no books. At that point, the ACLU had been brought in, and we got involved, along with a lot of other people throughout the state. The conditions in Eliezer's high school are terrible. The classrooms are very overcrowded. The bathrooms have no doors. There's no privacy. There's graffiti all over the place. You walk in there, it seems like the place has been forsaken. I know the lawsuit won't benefit Eliezer, but it will help other children. These are the future of our country, let alone our families. Also, I have a three-year-old daughter. I'm really keeping an eye on her education. We thought about homeschooling her but we can't do it. My wife and I both work. I've been thinking a lot about private school. When I was stationed in Texas, our older daughter was in private school through sixth grade. She is the only one of our children who graduated college. Going to private school made all the difference for her."

Pastor Williams's voice sinks into a lower register. "So far I haven't found a private school near us for my daughter. I don't want her to go through what Eliezer did. I'm not sure what to do."

•   •   •

Many public schools in our wealthiest suburbs and in booming cities such as Las Vegas feature facilities equal to any found in the most well-endowed private schools as well as classes that limit the number of students to a maximum of twenty. But as a former cochair of the board of trustees of a private school said, "Every school has a body and a soul. The body is the facilities, after-school programs, and so forth. The soul is the administration and staff, curriculum, and philosophy. You can be wowed by the body but I look for the soul."

The soul of every school is its faculty. Good teachers are rare; inspiring teachers are a gift. The best are adept communicators, innovative thinkers, and lifelong learners. They are not necessarily credentialed.

The dean of a private school, who began as a third grade teacher, graduated college with no thought at all of becoming a teacher. "I fell into it. I didn't know what I was going to do after college. I applied for a corporate job, didn't get it, then figured I'd follow my boyfriend to New York and look for a job there. One day, there was a job fair at school. I went and talked to the head of a private elementary school in New York. She described a dream job: working with kids, freedom to create your own curriculum, an inspiring work environment. I was hooked. Got the job and found my calling. I think that happens to a lot of people."

"Actually, we are the kids we teach," a middle school head told me. "We never want to leave school."

Many young college graduates, often from the Ivy League colleges, find a fit as private school teachers. Their background—as liberal arts graduates, high achievers with a passion for learning—flies against the stereotype associated with public school teachers: young people who have identified a career path in college and have graduated with a degree in education.

"There is nothing more meaningless than an education major," the middle school head said. "Those courses don't prepare you for the job. It's amazing. And there's nothing more suspicious than someone gushing, 'I got into teaching because I just *adore* kids!' That sends me running the other way. I want passionate, motivated, creative people. It goes without saying that they like kids. Why else would you apply for a job as an elementary school teacher?"

And what about the belief that public schools pay better than private schools?

"It's a myth," a school head told me. "We may not be able to offer the long-term security that a school district can because our teachers are not in a union, but as far as salary and benefit packages go, we're right up there. In fact, we might be pulling ahead."

• • •

Are private schools better than public schools?

The answer delves into the realm of judgment, that always dicey component required when assessing a *quality*. Some politicians and educators would argue that No Child Left Behind attempts to remove the qualitative component from the assessment process. Many educators would vehemently disagree, saying that you can't account for a child's mood on a given day, and that you can't test creativity, motivation, abstract reasoning ability, and collaboration skills, all cornerstones of progressive private school curriculums and factors that are the opposite of rote learning, which is what NCLB tests.

There is also a short answer to the question.

It depends on where you live and who you are.

Acknowledging that there are always exceptions, if you are poor, and especially if you are poor and live in a city, it is not out of bounds to say that any private school would be an improvement over your neighborhood school. Pastor Sweetie Williams participated in a lawsuit to try to improve sixty public schools across California, while his son Eliezer submitted himself to conditions in school every day that bordered on inhumane. But every case is not so clear-cut.

Eve, the daughter of a physician, lives in a wealthy suburb of a major city. She attended public school from kindergarten through twelfth grade. She received an excellent education and attends a top college.

Stacy, also the daughter of a physician, lives seven miles away from Eve in a desirable neighborhood in the city, but one where the public schools are decrepit, overcrowded, and a war zone for rival gangs. Having no choice, Stacy attended private schools from kindergarten through twelfth grade, and attends a top college.

In order to receive an education that approached Eve's in quality, Stacy's parents had to enroll her in private school. Their choices were either to pay close to $500,000 to educate her from kindergarten through twelfth grade or to move. Fortunately, Stacy's parents had the resources to afford to live where they wanted and provide Stacy with a quality education. Pastor Williams and millions like him simply do not have that option.

The four women I followed considered their local public schools. For each of them, this was the first step in their kindergarten application process. They came away with concerns about facilities, faculty, curriculum, class size, and safety. Only one mom, Lauren Pernice, who lives in an exclusive neighborhood, said that she would settle for public school should her son not be accepted to private school. The other three felt that getting their children into private school was nothing less than necessary.

• • •

The second reason parents apply to private school kindergarten, the second C—the belief that getting into the "right" kindergarten will put a child on the track to an elite college—at first seemed flimsy, if not downright absurd. I asked an educational consultant if her clients actually believe that getting into certain kindergartens will get their children into the Ivy League.

"I get calls like that every day," she said. "Had a call today from a woman who said, 'I want my kid to go to an Ivy League college. Where should he go to kindergarten?' The parents both went to Yale. And of course their child is *gifted*. First of all, I say to parents, 'It is your job to think that your child is gifted.' You have to be a cheerleader. Much better than saying, 'My child? Dumb shit.'"

When I asked Brianna, director of admissions at the elite Hunsford School, she just shook her head.

"The most incredible thing to me is how parents want to know if getting into our kindergarten, getting into Hunsford, will help you get into an elite college. Parents ask me that all the time. They always have. People with four-year-olds are asking this. They're very concerned. I find it astonishing. People think that if they don't do it right, their kid is not going to get into a name college. What is a name college? To them, it's a narrow little range of schools that are considered to be *elite*. The truth is we really don't think like that here. If you ask our teachers what we have our sights on, they will say they are trying to help form kids into fantastic people who will make a difference in the world. That means to us kind, thoughtful, caring, contributing human beings. There is a real disconnect between what educators see as necessary and what parents want. We are not basing this on air. We know what skill set causes children to become successful, and it's not what parents think it is. It is the ability to *collaborate*, to be part of a team. It's not the ability to sit and calculate all day long in a cubicle. It's communication skills. That's number one. The ability to look at problems and to imagine solutions that are not readily apparent. And first and foremost, it's about having confidence as a person. Esteem. Someday somebody will come up with an *E*Q test, esteem quotient, and that will be the end of IQ tests and ERBs and all of it. Parents just don't get it that kids who are pushed into those narrow little molds, kids who sometimes do brilliantly on all those tests, sometimes fail miserably in the world. It's because they don't know how to get along, they don't know how to do anything but deal with their own intellectual incredibleness. They don't know how to *think*."

Despite Brianna's plea for parents to change their focus to

their children's development rather than on getting them into a kindergarten that can lead them to an elite college, many prospective parents have college in their sights. Lauren Pernice expressed a common perspective.

"I probably shouldn't admit this, but when you're waiting in the admissions office to go on your tour, you flip through the brochure to see the list of where their high school graduates went to college. It's terrible but I'm looking for the Ivy Leagues. I am. I know we're talking about kindergarten but you want the *possibility.*"

Tony, a successful businessman, whose daughter currently attends an Ivy League university, put it even more directly: "I wanted to put her in a better position for college. I knew that the private school track would give her an edge, improve her odds, especially for an Ivy."

Then, anticipating the next question, he added, "If she had not gone to her private school, she would not have gotten in."

• • •

Tara is an independent college counselor. She guides high school seniors through the stressful college application process, editing their college essays, holding mock interviews, and helping fill out their applications. Tara charges a flat fee of $5,000 per client.

"There is a perception that certain schools, mostly elite private schools, have a more direct path into elite colleges," Tara said. "Everyone thinks: get your kid into the right kindergarten, which gets you into the right middle school and high school, and, bam, you're into the Ivy League. And because kindergarten is the main entry point there is this frenzy to get your kid in and put them on that track. It's not true that these colleges only take kids from these schools. But they do take the top kids.

The best colleges are looking for the best students. The valedictorian at Pemberley has a good chance of getting into an elite college. So does the valedictorian at Such and Such High in Fargo, North Dakota. In fact, the valedictorian at Such and Such High in Fargo, North Dakota, has a better chance of getting into Harvard than a kid from Pemberley who's not in the top ten percent of the class. Ultimately, it's about the caliber of student."

Is it? There is evidence that getting into a top college can sometimes be more about the school one attends than the student who applies. A college counselor at one of the country's top private high schools told me that the "top ten percent of our senior class gets into colleges with an Academic Reputation Rating, according to *U.S. News & World Report*, in the ninety-seventh percentile, while the students in the bottom ten percent go to colleges with an Academic Reputation Rating in the ninety-second percentile." These numbers directly contradict Tara: even the poorest students at the nation's top private schools get into excellent colleges.

There is no denying that there is a connection between the private school kindergarten track and getting into a top college. A report in the *Wall Street Journal*'s *Weekend Journal*, entitled "The Price of Admission" (April 2, 2004), calculated where the 2003 incoming freshman class at ten elite colleges—Brown, Cornell, Dartmouth, Duke, Harvard, Pomona, Princeton, the University of Chicago, the University of Pennsylvania, and Yale—went to high school. Using a criterion of having at least fifty students in the graduating class, the article ranked the schools that had the highest percentage of students admitted to those ten elite colleges. Of the top thirty high schools in the survey, twenty-nine were private schools, with tuition costs averaging well over

$20,000 per year. The one public high school that cracked the top thirty was Hunter College High School in New York City, an exclusive high school admitting only "gifted and talented" students. The article mentioned four other private high schools with graduating classes of fewer than fifty that except for class size would have topped the list. Adding these four, the scorecard reads thirty-three of thirty-four in favor of private schools. The article summed it up: "A number of the better-performing public schools were small, highly selective 'magnet' schools, meaning that students whose families live and pay taxes in the area don't necessarily get to attend. . . . Public schools were in the distinct minority."

. . .

Finally, there is the third *C*, country club, which is a euphemism meaning that parents want to get their children into certain private school kindergartens so that they can brag about this "achievement" at their country club or its social equivalent.

In other words, getting into the right kindergarten is all about *them*. It is a reflection of their excellence as people and their success as parents. Getting their child into the *right* kindergarten is similar to traveling in the *right* circle of friends, wearing the *right* labels, being seen at the *right* restaurant prior to making an appearance at the *right* charity event or opening night. After being turned down by Dana Optt, director of admissions at the prestigious Pemberley School, a distraught dad phoned her in a panic.

"What am I going to do?" he said. "My wife won't get out of bed. She says she can't show her face at the club."

Dana offered the perfect solution. "Tell her to say that you withdrew your application. Say the school wasn't for you. You want to support your public school instead. Or say I was a bitch in the interview. You can use me."

"That's good," the man said. "I'm going to do that."

"I tell people to do that all the time," Dana said. "Saves face."

"Thank you," the man said and hung up, satisfied, without ever uttering a word about his child, never even bothering to ask why he didn't get in.

All parents want their children to be happy, but as one educational consultant observed, happiness can be an emotion that they project onto their children.

"These parents say they want their kids to be happy, which means rich, a star in their field, and marrying well. They're wrong. That's what will make *them* happy. Because that means I, the parent, am successful, as opposed to accepting who your kid is. Does that come from getting into Harvard? Maybe. But I tend to think not."

•   •   •

It appears, sadly, that getting a quality education is no longer every child's right but a privilege reserved for the privileged. And the ranks of the privileged seem to be thinning out by the season.

Two directors of admissions bemoaned the fact that because of siblings and legacies they had only four kindergarten openings available. One school had exactly two openings.

"This year again we took only legacies and siblings," another admissions director said. "We did not have one single opening for anyone from the outside."

"Everything is amped up more than ever," said MK, Longbourne School's director of admissions. "For the first time that I can remember in New York, there was not a spot for every kid who applied. Many kids did not get in anywhere. Used to be, kids had choices. Now that happens less and less. There are many more kids than there are spaces."

The head of one of the nation's top private schools added, "People are applying to nine or ten schools, sometimes more, out of fear, the fear of not getting in somewhere. They want to be safe rather than sorry. That builds the anxiety until it starts to become a kind of hysteria. Think about writing ten applications, going on ten tours, having ten interviews. That takes an enormous amount of time and causes a ton of stress. It's crazy. It's like the parents are on a train. You go to the end of the train and there is college. Getting into this or that college is what drives things at secondary schools, which is driving the anxiety about elementary schools, which is driving the anxiety about nursery schools. The train starts at preschool and it never stops."

And now, bubbling below the surface of the kindergarten application process, looms a sinister factor that threatens the mental stability of prospective parents: the *sum* of the Three C's. While parents vie ferociously for a kindergarten spot, they know that not *any* spot will do. Their children's future is riding not just on *if* they get in, but *where*. An example in the extreme:

In 1999, in Tokyo, Mitsuko Yamada, a thirty-five-year-old nurse, kidnapped her neighbor's daughter from a nursery school playground, forced her into a public restroom, and strangled her with a scarf. Four days later, overcome with grief and shame, Yamada turned herself in to the police. Sobbing uncontrollably, she confessed that she had killed the child out of jealousy. The child had gotten into a better kindergarten than her daughter had. The little girl's mother had begun to brag and Yamada could no longer take it.

The subsequent trial caused a media storm in Japan, resulting in a series of local newspaper articles about Yamada, her daily life, and her relationship with the other mothers in the school. The newspaper reported that it had received more than a thousand letters, faxes, and e-mails . . . in *support* of Yamada.

To my knowledge, no one in America has actually killed to get their child into kindergarten.

Yet.

CHAPTER TWO

Meet the Parents

I know that when parents visit a school, they're looking for a vibe. Well, so are we. If we don't get it, we won't accept.

—a private school director of admissions

Private School Expo

In most cities, the kindergarten application season begins two weeks after it ends. While scores of parents are on edge, waiting to hear if their children will be accepted off waitlists, new armies of prospective kindergarten applicants mass at the borders of private school auditoriums and gymnasiums, ransack tables piled high with information packets and admissions brochures, and thrust themselves onto school heads and directors of admissions, attempting to create indelible impressions of themselves to combat the cold, unfamiliar names that lie merely handwritten or printed on thousands of application forms.

They are at war.

. . .

The Darcy School is a city school, vertical in design, layered like a massive concrete wedding cake. Entering the school through twin metal gates, you walk through a lush courtyard resembling the lobby of a Vegas hotel, which leads into a combination theater and gymnasium with a freshly burnished hardwood floor. The gym sits below two levels of classrooms, an art studio and music room, computer and science labs, capped by an enclosed rooftop playground.

But one night each April, the Darcy School gymnasium morphs from an elite private elementary school into a mini–convention center and host of "Private School Expo" or "Kindergarten Presentation Night," as the heading reads on the half-inch-thick handout each attendee receives. Below the heading, the handout announces a list of more than forty participating schools. Each school fills a full page, its vital information clumped in dense, size-ten-font paragraphs: address, telephone, e-mail, Web site, contact person, year founded, religious affiliation, dress code, mission statement, ethnic diversity, and under separate headings, description of the application/enrollment process, including but not limited to projected openings for kindergarten. Three words in bold black letters top the final paragraph—**Tuition and Fees**—followed by ominous, insistent, and ludicrous numbers, resulting in sticker shock for even the most well-heeled in attendance.

Flipping through the school descriptions, the shock evolves into a sense of dread. Paying for school is one thing; being admitted is quite another. Skimming the breakdown of the applications to Meryton, among the most difficult schools in the city to get into, you read, "Projected openings for kindergarten: 26."

Meryton typically receives three to four hundred kindergarten applications. Of the twenty-six projected openings, siblings, legacies, and children of faculty will, in a conservative estimate, nab the first ten, reducing the available openings to sixteen. If Meryton hits its high-end projection of four hundred applications, the odds of being accepted are a daunting twenty-five to one.

.   .   .

Tonight, school heads and admissions directors representing the forty private schools stand at card tables that rim the perimeter of the gym. The schools are arranged in alphabetical order beginning on the left side. Each table is covered with brochures and application packets piled high in front of a sign announcing the name of the school in green cursive handwriting. The Expo has not yet begun but there are already two hundred parents massed outside the gymnasium doors. Once the doors open, a steady flow of incoming traffic promises to double that number within the half hour.

Dana Optt, director of admissions at Pemberley School, mid-forties, a shade under six feet tall, her hair snowball white and spectacularly large, prepares for the siege. Her first hint of the upcoming onslaught begins while she is arranging brochures in four neat rows on her table. As she finishes laying out the first row, two handsome men in their thirties appear. One is African American, the other Asian. They wear matching charcoal gray suits. To Dana's trained eye, they look as if they work out.

"Excuse us," the Asian man says. "I'm Howard and this is Lionel."

Lionel smiles. "We don't mean to bother you, but we knew if we didn't catch you now, we'd probably never get a chance to talk to you."

Dana returns his smile. "You guys are good. They haven't opened the doors yet. How'd you get in here?"

"We're very convincing," Howard says.

"So you want your kid to go to Pemberley," Dana says. "Okay. Convince me."

That's all it takes—Dana's razor sharpness and her absolute intolerance for bullshit—and the three of them lose it.

"Hurry up now," Dana says through her laugh. "I'm gonna be swamped by a million people in two minutes."

"Well, admitting us helps us and you," Lionel says.

"How so?"

"Pemberley is the best school in the city and same-sex couples are *in*."

"Look at us," Howard says. "You've got all your diversity covered in one family."

"Honey, we are dripping in diversity," Lionel says.

Dana laughs again. "You guys are a trip."

"I don't care what they're selling in the red states," Howard says. "We are the wave of the future."

"We're the perfect couple," Lionel says, dipping his head onto Howard's shoulder. "We have money. We will be involved in our child's education, in every way. We're very generous with our time and our resources."

"You're ringing every bell," Dana says. "I'm taking a guess. Who's the lawyer in the family?"

"You're good," Howard says. "I am. Real estate. Big button-down firm downtown. I'm the token goy."

"I'm a recovering investment banker," Lionel says. "I stay at home with the kid."

"Tell me about the kid."

Ridiculously, spontaneously, Lionel and Howard gush.

"Where do we start?" Howard says. "Justin is beautiful, curious, funny, sweet . . . did I say beautiful?"

Dana winks at them. "You forgot to tell me how smart he is. He's gifted, right?"

"God, I hope not," Howard says. "I just hope he's normal."

"Like us," says Lionel.

Dana roars. "You guys are too much."

"Oh, just wait, honey," Lionel says. "If there's an issue at school, I can get as bitchy as any country club princess."

The doors to the gymnasium open with a rumble and the floor literally begins to shake. Within ten seconds, a throng of humanity stampedes inside, thirty parents on a torpedo line, headed right for Dana.

"We won't take up any more of your time," Howard says. "We just wanted to introduce ourselves."

"What Howard means is that we wanted to fawn all over you, make an indelible impression, bond, and tell you that you're even more fabulous than your reputation."

"And that's the truth. We're not just sucking up," Howard says.

"You're too funny," Dana says. "Listen, I'm dying to meet Justin. Call my office, come to the open house, and we'll go from there."

"So when we say Howard and Lionel are calling, you'll remember?"

"I think I will," Dana says.

•   •   •

Lauren and Craig Pernice live in a cavernous two-story Tudor built into the base of a hill in one of the most desirable neighborhoods in the city. The rooms in their house are vast and open. They own few pieces of furniture but what they do have is overstuffed and oversized: an enormous L-shaped couch planted in front of a mammoth plasma-screen TV in a family room dotted with DVDs, kids' toys, art projects, and sporting equipment; a walk-in refrigerator dominated by a wall of diet peach Snapple in a football field of a kitchen; expansive children's bedrooms with built-in desks along entire walls, framed by jumbo bunk beds; and a master bedroom with a super-size canopy bed, a multiplex movie theater–size screen across the way, floor to ceiling. The Pernice house feels, in the best sense, *lived* in, especially by their two sons, Killian, four, and Joseph, two. Craig, steady, calm, tall, guarded, is a partner in an investment banking firm that specializes in deals relating to the environment. In the business world, he is known as a player, a role model for newly matriculated MBAs. Lauren, she is fond of saying, is Craig's flip side: excitable, passionate, petite, formerly a graduate student in Russian literature at Harvard, currently a stay-at-home mom. Lauren is between careers, grappling with life choices now that she has some time on her hands. She is open about discussing this but wonders if she is saying too much. She laughs nervously and admits that she just can't censor herself. Lauren speaks machine-gun fast in a soft Virginia drawl, the result of her Charlottesville childhood; if you don't home in, you can easily miss the heart of her conversation.

"Killian's got tremendously strong academics but some social needs," she says one afternoon curled up on the couch in the family room. "Going into kindergarten he'll be reading chapter books. And his math is very developed."

She combs her fingers through her jet black hair, cut short with tight bangs, resembling a stylish helmet. Lauren wears glasses, black wraparound Calvin Kleins, tapered so that they obscure her eyes. "Frankly, I have some concerns that there is so much money in the secular private schools in this city. I am not as comfortable in that medium as Craig is. Obviously we do very well. Craig makes a good living. We're very lucky. But it's not the background I came from. Everything's a trade-off, I recognize that. You can't have it all. It's just that at these schools there's the Prada vibe floating around and it's kind of a sticking point for me."

She peers at the ceiling as if checking for leaks.

"Maybe that's hypocritical, I don't know. Whatever the setting, we want strong academics side by side with true emotional and social development. At least that's our ideal."

Lauren changes position, pretzels herself so that she can see her yard through the family room window. "We've decided to apply to Pemberley School. That's really our one and only choice. And I can say how we became interested in Pemberley in two words: Dana Optt."

Lauren shakes her short hair as if it's still wet from a shower.

"Amazing lady. She is so physically imposing. Plus I would not want to play Scrabble against her. She's very sharp. And she gets right to it. Pemberley wasn't on our radar until we went to the Private School Expo thing. There were a ton of people crowding around the Pemberley table. Dana was describing the school, the curriculum, the philosophy, and it sounded like the best of all possible worlds. We kind of hung back, waited until we saw an opening, and then squeezed our way up to her. We introduced ourselves and I described Killian. I said, 'He's very bright, academically quite advanced, but socially could really benefit by working with his peers.'"

Lauren pokes a finger into the air as if testing the wind. "Actually the specific question we asked was, 'What are the opportunities for collaborative learning? We think Killian would get a lot out of doing group projects. I think that's an important skill for him to develop.'

"And Dana said, 'We do a lot of that at Pemberley. We choose the kids carefully for the collaborative projects. We'll put one of the kids who's very bright with one of the kids who's maybe more social. It drives the bright kids nuts because they want to do it all themselves.' That spoke to us. Craig said, 'So, our kid, like the kid you described, he's not that unusual.' And Dana looked at him and she said, rather gently, 'No. He's not unusual at all.'

"It was Dana's response," Lauren says softly. "Her sensitivity. The way she described it, like they've been there. I'm definitely going to their open house, to really look at Pemberley. It sounds like they've had kids like Killian. Because she said he's, I mean . . ."

Ambushed by a surprise catch in her throat, she swallows, and says, quietly, "She said . . . he's not so unusual."

New York Mom

Jennifer Shea Cohen, thirty-three, lives on the twenty-first floor of a prewar building just off Park Avenue. She wears her red hair shoulder-length and straight and is dressed in black jeans and a black sweater. Her eyes form steel blue pools, and when she smiles her upper lip curls to the left as though she's not sure she should go all the way with it. In the fifth grade, friends started calling her Shea to distinguish her from the two other Jennifers in her class. Now few people outside of her family know her as anything but Shea.

Shea steps into her living room and flashes the turned-up smile. She has furnished the room in art deco, including a neon green couch and two matching green chairs. A large plasma TV is mounted on a wall next to a picture window that overlooks Park Avenue.

"We love it here," Shea says. "I can't imagine raising our kids anywhere but in the city."

Shea and her husband, Donald, are lifelong New Yorkers. Shea grew up on the Upper West Side, her dad a Columbia professor, her mom a freelance editor. Donald grew up in Greenwich Village, the son of a banker and a stay-at-home mom who gave piano lessons on the side. Donald inherited both of his parents' professions: he works full-time as a financial analyst and moonlights as the piano player in a jazz trio. Recently, the trio recorded a CD, which they sell over the Internet. Shea works part-time in marketing for a well-known national charity.

"Donald and I met at the University of Michigan. There we were, these two New Yorkers, away at school, meeting at a fraternity party. It was funny. We both wanted to move back to New York, find good jobs, raise a family, and live on the Upper East Side. Probably doesn't sound very romantic but that's what we wanted. We went for it. Here we are."

Below on Park Avenue, a car horn blares. It is the last week of April and Shea has already begun the application process for private school, sixteen months before her son, Liam, will begin kindergarten.

"I want to get all this stuff in early. I work, I have two kids. I have a lot on my plate. I'm going to write the essay over the summer and have it ready to go. The first step, really, is you have to know your kid. There are a lot of people who know the schools better than they know their own children. They don't consider the fit. In New York, you start by asking, coed or single-sex? Now, for Liam, who is a bright kid but also a very creative spirit, I'm looking for a school that will foster creativity within a structured environment. Most single-sex schools tend to be a bit more formal, which sometimes goes against the idea of being creative. Not always. For me, it's about finding that right school and going for it. I'm the type of person who gets focused on one or two places rather than, 'Oh my God, I'd be so happy if he got into any one of six schools.'"

Shea flicks on a chrome floor lamp standing in the corner. "We went on a tour of Longbourne earlier this week. That's all boys but we absolutely loved it. Very into the arts, music, theater. The kids wear uniforms and it's very academic but you get a real nurturing feel in the classroom. A lot of shared tables, not desks in rows. Young teachers really engaging with the kids. Tons of art on the walls. Outside the classroom there isn't such an emphasis on athletics, the way it is at a lot of other boys' schools. I could really see Liam there. We'd be thrilled if he got in. But altogether we're applying to, let's see—"

Shea ticks the numbers off on her fingers. "Seven total. This is New York. That's a reasonable number." She stands. "Let me get my chart." She heads out of the room, tosses over her shoulder, "I'm very organized."

A sound of a drawer opening and closing in the kitchen and Shea is back, holding a computer printout. She settles onto the couch. "I made a chart that lists the schools. I have a little column that says *application*."

She points to a header on the page. The chart is color-coded, pale neon hues matching her living room decor: lime green, soft pink, pale blue.

"Then I have a column here that I will update when I call the school, and when I receive the application. I mark it *received*. Then when I finish writing it, I mark it *finished*, and then finally I mark it *mailed* and the date. I have this in my computer at work so I can update it as the process goes along. Here I have marked these *called* and so on. And then I have a column for *tour, our interview,* and *Liam's interview,* and on that I put the date and the person who gives us the tour. That way I'm all set when I write the thank-you note. Got the person's name. Voilà."

She tosses herself backward into the couch. "Donald's a little intimidated by my chart." Shea shrugs. "I can't help it." She leans forward abruptly, points at the chart. "I'd love to be able to strategize a little when it comes to Liam's interviews but we may not have a choice. Our thought is to try to hedge, if we can. In other words, we're going to try not to make Longbourne his first interview. A lot of people say, 'Don't have what you think is your favorite school be his first one.' I don't think it'll matter to Liam. Unless he's having some meltdown day, but that's not even in his personality. And the interviews vary. Some of them are little group interviews. Some are one-on-one. I know at this one school the woman who interviews the kids has a reputation of being kind of out there. We hear she does odd things. I heard from a friend that she made her son jump up and down on one foot. Not sure what she was going for. Maybe looking to see if the kid had physical issues."

Shea leans forward, steeples her fingers on her knees. "I know it's a crazy thing, this process. The competition is terrible. In our small corner of the world there are not only all these smart kids, there is this concentration of well-educated, success-ful, competitive parents who are pushing, really *pushing*. I am try-ing not to get caught up in all this. But it's hard. A lot of these ultra-competitive parents start by pushing their kids into these feeder nursery schools where the directors are connected to the ongoing schools. Liam's school is a little off the radar. Our di-rector is kind of connected, but the school is not known as a feeder. That's okay. You have to draw the line somewhere. You start thinking, is it really worth it to pay $15,000 for nursery school where your kid is basically playing in the sand all day? I guess the argument is that the feeder schools spend more time preparing the kids for the ERB tests. That's a whole other issue. But you can do that at home. Read to your kid, play Candyland, play Mighty Mind games or things like that. It's a vicious cycle."

Falling in Love

Katie Miller is about to fall in love.

Deeply, madly, desperately in love.

The emotion hits her without warning, a sneak attack. The wave of feeling begins suddenly in the Hunsford School parking lot.

"Look at this," Katie says, indicating the clock on the dashboard in her SUV. "From my driveway to the school, seven minutes. For someone who lives in her car, that is a major plus. Now, where do I park?"

On cue, a uniformed security guard appears at Katie's driver-side window. He holds a clipboard. He beams. "Good morning."

Katie smiles back. "Good morning."

"Here for the tour?"

"Yes." She nods at the clipboard. "Katie Miller."

"Right here." He flicks at her name with a fingertip and grins again. "Just pull into any one of those spaces."

"Thank you."

Katie chooses an open space at the end of the lot. "I'm glad it's self-parking. I know you pay a lot for private school but I'm thinking, Hunsford has valet parking? That's a bit much."

She climbs down from her SUV while simultaneously checking to make sure she's armed with her notebook and two pens. Today Katie wears a light blue cashmere sweater and pale jeans, a sunnier, less somber look than the outfit she wore recently for her public school tour. Katie is a force of nature, a five-foot, dark-haired packet of purpose and energy. Look around the room to see who's in charge and you will inevitably find Katie.

Katie strides toward the school, her pace at redline. The security guard leans back on his heels and points through a black wire gate. "You'll be going to the multipurpose room, the blue door on your right."

"Thanks," Katie says.

"You're welcome. Enjoy Hunsford." His smile broadens. He presses a button inside a metal box behind his head. The gate grunts once and swings open with a clang and Katie enters the campus of Hunsford School.

As the gate clatters behind her, Katie stops. She is instantly struck silent and still by what she sees before her: an open grassy area dotted with small overhanging trees adding occasional shade and a delicate, strangely mystical aura; park benches of varnished wood spaced along a winding concrete pathway; the aroma of eucalyptus and mint, thick, sweet, nurturing, persistent; and a cluster of buildings, immaculate yet lived-in A-frames on the perimeter of the parklike grounds giving a sense of, well, Katie can't quite put her finger on it. There is, ironically, no sense of *school*. Instead Katie feels something else, something . . . larger. She feels an immense *calm*. Contentment. And then it hits her. It's as if she has wandered through some kind of enchanted garden and has come home. That's what Hunsford feels like.

Home.

For the next thirteen years.

"I'm in love," Katie says.

She steps forward dizzily, then rights herself, realizing that she's in search of the multipurpose room, where the tour will begin.

"Blue door," she mumbles, and veers off to the first building on her right. She opens the door.

Inside the blue door, twenty prospective parents, all dressed *up*, women in suits attached to men in suits, mingle, juggling plastic coffee cups. Most of the men looked dazed, distracted. The women appear hungry, eager, on the prowl, mining for clues, digging for information, pining to connect with three other women stationed at strategic locations throughout the room. Two of those women are dressed formally, women who lunch, except for nametags identifying them as "Assistant Director of Admissions" and "President, PA." The third woman, Brianna, wears a floor-length smock in a muted earth tone. Her nametag reads, "Director of Admissions."

"I thought I was early," Katie mutters. The PA president, spying Katie with a point guard's peripheral vision, splits off from her conversation and extends a long pale arm. "Welcome to Hunsford. I'm Miranda Gary, president of the Parents' Association."

"Katie Miller." Katie shakes Miranda's hand. She encloses Miranda's fingers tightly, conscious of not wanting her first Hunsford handshake to be moist and fishy. No need. Miranda's grip is strong, full of confidence and Pilates.

"So glad to meet you." Miranda's smile is genuine, warm, doesn't feel practiced. "Grab some coffee, a bagel, some fruit, and if you have any questions about how parents become involved here at Hunsford, please feel free to ask. I know you've probably already heard a lot on the *street*"—and here Miranda extricates her hand from Katie's and makes imaginary quotation marks in the air, something Katie usually finds incredibly annoying—"but Hunsford is truly a community. We *want* parents to be involved. You are a partner in your child's education."

"I couldn't agree more," Katie says. "A lot of schools want you to hang back a little, or so I've heard, but I want to help in any way I can. In the classroom, on field trips, community service, I think that's so important—"

"If everyone would take a seat, we'll get started." Brianna's voice. Barely above a whisper but somehow commanding. The din in the room collapses as prospective parents scramble to find chairs around a long metal conference table.

"We'll continue this conversation later," Miranda whispers. She brushes Katie's shoulder with the palm of her hand and offers a final smile, one of promise. At least that's how Katie interprets her look. Katie smiles back and mouths, "Okay."

There is one seat left at the table, at the far end, directly across from Brianna. Katie eases into the seat and smiles at Brianna, who meets the smile with a slight, conspiratorial nod. Katie feels herself blush, as if she is in high school and the boy she has a crush on has noticed her staring at him. She drops her eyes and peeks at the other parents around the table to see if anyone has noticed her suddenly crimson cheeks. To her relief, everyone is focused on Brianna, their attention rapt, undivided, devoted to her as if she were their cult leader.

"Welcome to Hunsford," Brianna says.

The parents respond in group-speak, ranging from the guttural to one woman's unfortunate outburst, "Glad to be here!" The other parents laugh, as does Brianna, who rescues the moment and the woman by saying, simply, "Well, I'm glad you're here, too."

She then allows silence to blanket the room as she folds her hands on the table in front of her. She waits. Her eyes are focused front, straight at Katie, and Katie wonders now if she's sitting in a bad spot. She has to look at Brianna, has to keep eye contact, has to be her focus, because at no point does Brianna look away, disengage, offer her any relief. Brianna speaks now, her eyes locked onto Katie's.

"Let me explain what will happen this morning. I am going to give you a brief description of Hunsford, tell you what we're about, describe our school, our philosophy, our facilities, our curriculum, our kids, and the Hunsford community, and then you will go on a tour, led by one of our parent volunteers. After the tour, you'll return here and you'll have an opportunity to ask questions. But because time is short, please save your questions until then. I promise you'll have plenty of time to have all your questions answered. Okay?"

Katie nods, Brianna's partner, her shill, and then, for the first time, she unlocks her eyes from Brianna's as she fumbles inside her purse in search of a pen and her notepad. She locates them, pulls them out, flips the notebook open to a blank page and smooths it out with the palm of her hand. When she looks up, Brianna's eyes are gone, fastened like lasers into those of the balding, pale man next to her, who blinks back from beneath a butterscotch-colored unibrow. Katie feels oddly jilted.

She shakes it off. Brianna begins talking about Hunsford in a slow, almost musical lilt. She has, of course, offered up this information a thousand times before, but her low, whispery speech pattern makes everything about the school, even its ungodly acceptance numbers, sound seductive. Brianna segues into the developmental philosophy behind Hunsford, which she describes as a "devotion to providing a stress-free, yet academic atmosphere while embracing each child in a nurturing little blanket geared toward allowing learning at one's own pace and promoting gobs of self-esteem.

"There is no one right way," Brianna assures the parents before her, spreading her arms like two delicate wings. "We've just found that *this* way has worked for us . . . and we're beginning our twenty-fifth year."

For some reason, perhaps to ease the encroaching tension in the room, this pronouncement breaks everybody up. Brianna allows herself a tiny giggle in chorus with her audience.

"All right then, why don't we divide into smaller groups and tour Hunsford? Let's see, everybody on my left, you'll go with Allison, and those on my right, go with Miranda."

And where does that leave me? Katie wonders, a teeny wave of panic rising into her throat. *I'm right smack-dab in front of you.* She pokes her hand up between a raise and a salute.

"I'm not sure if I'm on your right or your left."

The words rush from Katie unchecked, tucked into a breathy, uncomfortable giggle. Brianna's eyebrows tepee. Suddenly, happily, she laughs along with Katie. "I see your problem." Then, without hesitation, calls, "Miranda, take Katie in your group."

Katie tilts her head girlishly, allowing a broad smile, and walks over to a dozen parents swarming around Miranda Gary, Hunsford Parents' Association president.

"Hi again," Miranda gushes.

"Hi," Katie says, accompanied by a tiny piano wave of her fingers. But as she follows the group out of the multipurpose room onto the Hunsford campus, all she can think is, *She knows my name. The director of admissions at Hunsford knows my name.*

•   •   •

The tour itself is magical, as wondrous as Katie's first cruise through the melodic and somnolent "It's a Small World" ride at Disneyland when she was five or six. Like the ride's repetitive, addictive song, the music of Hunsford sticks in your head. And like Disneyland, there is joy here at Hunsford. Katie experiences it everywhere: in the faces of the kindergarten children watched over by *two* full-time credentialed teachers, one young, pretty, exuberant, the other slightly older, sturdier, more motherly; in the eyes of the teachers themselves, burning with intelligence and commitment and the sheer pleasure of teaching these adorable, spongelike, lucky little ones; in the artwork on the walls, splashes of color and imagination and confidence; in the games played in the grassy, open physical education area, games unrestricted by competition, Miranda explains, games defined by sharing and collaboration and good sportsmanship; in the music room, where unrestricted fugues of experimentation crash through the walls without regard to form; in the snapshots she sees of mind-bending computer art, photography, science, geography, even *math*. ("We teach math at Hunsford as a living, breathing organism. Numbers are *alive*.") In sum, as Katie walks through Hunsford, her mouth agape, her eyes on the verge of watering, she feels the joy of *learning*. To her mind, Hunsford is what school should be.

Katie then makes a decision. Steadily but imperceptibly, as if she is running a race and trailing the pack, she starts to move up from her position at the rear of her tour group until she squeezes ahead of them all and is walking side by side with Miranda. Katie doesn't care if anyone else notices. She knows—or at least she's been told—two things: when you see your school, you'll know it, and once you know it, do everything in your power to get in.

It's on, Katie thinks. *Right now.* I'm going to start by making myself known to the Parents' Association president. As cochair of the PTA at Alex's preschool, Katie is aware of how certain things operate. She is aware, for example, that she has a powerful voice, a voice that will be heard if she wants a particular family admitted to Bright Stars, her daughter's preschool. Of course, she has no ultimate control over who will be accepted and who will not. But she knows that her opinion matters to Gracie, director of Bright Stars. She knows that Gracie and Brianna talk and if Katie wants Hunsford, it's important to get Gracie on her side as soon as possible. Having fallen in love, Katie wastes no time in going for the kill.

Miranda stops the tour at a third grade classroom. She tiptoes two feet in, locates a chubby ten-year-old in pigtails, and blows her a kiss. The little girl hunches her shoulders in a shrug. Miranda backs into the hall and resumes the tour.

"My daughter," she says.

Katie sighs. "She seems so happy."

"She loves it here. She's made so many friends, and unlike some of the more *academic* schools"—fingers up again with those cloying air quotes—"that load you down with three hours of homework a night, she has a *life*."

"Three hours of homework a night? In third grade?"

Miranda shakes her head solemnly. "That's what you hear."

Katie dips her head within an inch of Miranda's shoulder. By now, they are five feet ahead of the rest of the tour, fast friends, conspirators.

"Which schools?" Katie whispers.

"Meryton, Darcy, Pemberley."

"I think that's cruel."

Miranda shakes her head again, this time in agreement. "Not to mention the fact that they give *grades*."

Now it's Katie's turn to shake her head while Miranda shrugs. "Different strokes for different folks."

"Not what *I'd* want to pay for," Miranda murmurs.

· · ·

An hour later, after the tour, as the parents file into the multipurpose room for the question-and-answer session with Brianna, Katie boldly asks Miranda if they can exchange e-mail addresses. "I feel so comfortable here," Katie explains.

As Miranda fumbles through her purse for a business card, Katie senses hesitation, as if she has misread her connection with Miranda. Perhaps she's overeager, becoming too familiar too soon.

"That's okay," Katie says. "I didn't mean to impose."

Miranda yanks her hand out of her purse as if she's burned it. "I don't really e-mail."

"You'll probably see me soon enough anyway," Katie says, attempting to salvage the moment with a laugh. "I'll be back with my husband."

"So you're the scout, huh?"

"Yep," Katie says. "I scout the schools, then bring Miles if I like a place."

"I did the same thing," Miranda says. "Paul wouldn't give up a morning of work unless I fell in love."

"I'm right there," Katie says. "I'm in love."

Miranda beams. Katie smiles.

Back on track.

· · ·

In the question-and-answer session, Katie asks two questions: "Is Spanish part of the Hunsford curriculum?" ("Yes. We have a full-time Spanish teacher. The children take Spanish three times a week, starting in third grade.") And "Where do the kids eat when it rains?" which earns an "Excellent question" from Brianna and a supportive smile from Miranda. ("The children eat in their classrooms with their teachers. It's very fun.")

After exactly one hour, Brianna stands and excuses herself, turning the rest of the session over to her second in command, a tall, wild-haired woman named Fontaine. Miraculously, the parents have no more questions, preferring instead to encircle Brianna before she exits. Katie decides to hang back and take her time packing up. She has no intention of leaving Hunsford anonymously, just another face in the crowd. Besides, in truth, she likes it here. She wants to soak everything in, allow the vibe to remain as long as possible. She slowly makes her way to the door, past a trio of Prada-clad desperate housewives hovering around Brianna like vultures, their husbands long gone. As Katie slides by the group, Brianna points a finger in the air and calls to her. "Thanks for coming, Katie. I look forward to meeting Miles and Alex."

"Thank you," Katie says. "I loved it."

But she is stunned that Brianna knows not just her name but her husband's and her daughter's names as well and that she made a point of saying good-bye to her. *Either I made an impression or she's really good at this,* Katie thinks. *It's probably both.*

Katie steps out of the multipurpose room. She takes one last look at the inviting, grassy area in front of her. She feels a sudden twinge of sadness and longing, almost as if she is watching a lover step onto a train en route to a faraway, unknown destination. She turns and is face-to-face with Miranda.

"It was so nice meeting you, Katie," Miranda says.

"Likewise," Katie says. "You're a wonderful tour guide."

"Oh, thanks. I try." Miranda pauses, then hands Katie her business card. "My e-mail address. In case you have any questions."

Katie's lip curls up in surprise and then, spontaneously, they hug.

CHAPTER THREE

Front of the Brochure

Every applicant needs a hook. Something that distinguishes you. But I do think the nice, normal, middle-of-the-road family who in the long run would bring a lot to a school gets overlooked.

—*a private school director of admissions*

Ethnic diversity does matter. Especially if the family can pay.

—*a director of admissions, spoken with no awareness of irony*

A Question of Balance

Does diversity matter?

Do admissions directors seek to create balanced, diversified kindergarten classes? Does being a child of *distinction*, as one school refers to ethnic diversity, give an applicant an edge? Or are most private schools bastions of ethnic and economic homogeneity?

"Our admissions committee has a list of criteria for each year," one admissions director told me. "We look at girl-boy ratio, the financial aspect, ethnic diversity, and geographical diversity. We like to think that people come from all over the place."

The euphemism for diversity, repeated dozens of times by most private school directors of admissions and heads of school, is *balance*. "We're going for balance," said Dana Optt, director of admissions at Pemberley School. "This year I took eight diversity kids. I know I won't get all of them. I'll be happy if I get five."

Balance, of course, does not mean equality. While Dana and other well-meaning directors of admissions seem genuinely concerned about incorporating children of ethnic diversity into their incoming kindergarten mix, the fact is that private schools such as Pemberley remain steadfastly white.

"We try," said Dana, a hint of sadness and frustration in her voice. "But we exist in a different world. We are very far geographically and culturally from the inner city. I try to reach out but I need help."

•   •   •

According to an article entitled "Choosing the Right Private School for Your Kids," published in *Black Enterprise* magazine, "More and more African-American parents have concluded that the nation's public schools are failing to meet their children's needs" and "more and more black parents are pursuing private school options." The article lists three reasons for African-American parents' increasing interest in applying to private schools: "Parents want to escape the crime and mediocre education of some public schools"; "They seek an enriched curriculum for their high-achieving youngsters"; and "They demand a rigorous education to increase their children's chances of getting into a good college." The article appeared in October 1994. Since then things have not changed.

Over the past twenty years, several organizations have sprung up across the country to help guide minority students and their parents through every step of the process, from filling out the application and the often daunting financial aid forms to helping with acculturation once a child is accepted. Among the cities served by such organizations as A Better Chance, Early Steps, Prep for Prep, and the Independent School Alliance for Minority Affairs are New York, Boston, Washington, D.C., and Los Angeles.

"Since its inception in 1984, the Alliance has placed nearly two thousand kids in private schools," says Manasa Tangalin, executive director of the Alliance for Minority Affairs.

Ms. Tangalin explained that the Alliance serves as both a recruiting institution and a support system. Applicants pay a flat forty-five-dollar fee for a common application that is sent to as many of the forty member schools as an applicant chooses. Alliance workers also help applicants arrange for interviews at the schools and advise them which private schools seem like an appropriate match. Once they are accepted, the results are astounding: one hundred percent of graduating seniors from the Alliance have gone on to college. And the list of colleges that accepted these students is impressive: more than a hundred kids have attended such elite colleges as Harvard, Yale, Princeton, Dartmouth, Brown, Penn, Columbia, Cornell, Stanford, Amherst, Duke, Georgetown, Rice, and the University of Chicago. Would a hundred percent of those students have gone on to college if they had stayed in public school?

Manasa Tangalin says no.

•   •   •

Some concerned citizens are attacking the issue of racial imbalance in private schools with a radical, innovative approach. The article "A Private School Tackles the Racial Gap," published in the *New York Times* on November 24, 2005, describes how donors connected to St. George's, a private elementary school located in a wealthy Memphis suburb, presented school officials $6 million to create a sister school in the city, eight miles away. The experiment began in 1999 in a renovated church with the creation of St. George's Memphis. By September 2005, St. George's Memphis had enrolled nearly a hundred children from pre-kindergarten through second grade, with the expectation of adding a grade a year, stopping at fifth grade. Most of the children come from black and Hispanic working-class families. Parents must pay a minimum of $500 a year, with the rest subsidized by scholarships. The first year the new director of admissions recruited children by knocking on doors in the neighborhood. Six years later, there are more applicants than openings.

With the goal of narrowing the achievement gap academically and bridging social differences, both schools share the same lesson plans and some of the same teachers and join each other for field trips, community service projects, and social events. In 2009, the first fifth grade class from St. George's Memphis will combine with its sister school in the suburbs to form an integrated sixth grade in a new middle school.

Early indications suggest that the experiment is working. Tests given to second graders showed that all but two of the twenty children at St. George's Memphis were reading more than a half year above grade level, only slightly less than their suburban counterparts who were reading just above third grade level. School officials believe that by fifth grade, test scores will indicate virtually no difference between the two schools. Perhaps with an eye on Memphis, private schools in Cincinnati and Philadelphia have begun similar experiments.

• • •

Then there is the opposite extreme: private schools that resist the issue of diversity altogether. New York mom Shea Cohen recalled a panel discussion held at her preschool one evening in May.

"It was made up of parents whose kids go to the various schools in Manhattan. They would describe the schools and you could ask questions. I started getting more of a feel for the different schools that night. What we liked, what turned us off."

Shea smiled her Drew Barrymore upward tilt.

"So we're at this meeting." She covered her mouth with her fist. "This is unbelievable. There is a school called Hurst Academy. It's incredibly WASPy. Every little boy is blond and every mother is blonde and wispy and willowy, like Buffy. This mom in our class, an African-American woman, asks, 'How much diversity is there at your school?' And the Hurst Academy woman goes, 'None. We have no diversity. Zero. Sorry. It is what it is.' There was a gasp, followed by dead silence in the room, but the woman was so honest, it was both shocking and actually hysterical. So that was easy. Cross Hurst off our list."

• • •

Finally, regrettably, I encountered more than one school official whose attitude toward ethnic diversity approached the purely promotional. I asked Nan F., director of admissions at Darcy, one of the most exclusive private schools in the city, "When it comes to diversity, do you look for anything in particular?"

"Well." She paused, peeked at my tape recorder, shrugged. "We took these African-American twins last year who were . . . actually, who cares what they were . . . they were *gorgeous*. You thought, 'Brochure! Front of the brochure!'"

"Is that why you took them?"

Nan fixed me with a crooked, bemused smile. "Honey, *everybody* took them."

Nametag Recognition

The first week in May, on a brilliantly clear and unseasonably warm Thursday evening, Pemberley School hosts the first of its half-dozen open houses and parent tours. Pemberley is located on a hill above the city, lording over one of its most expensive and exclusive neighborhoods. The school's entrance is hidden from the main road, up a winding gravel drive through a mini-forest until, incongruously, two towering iron gates emerge and block your way. The only indication that you have arrived at Pemberley is the metal call box emblazoned with a crimson red crest and cursive *P* in its center.

Katie Miller, at the wheel of her SUV, and her friend Trina D'Angelo, riding shotgun, pull up behind a BMW convertible and wait their turn to enter the Pemberley grounds. They have driven past the gravel entry road twice, but, heeding the word on the street that finding Pemberley is every prospective parent's first challenge, they factored in extra time to get lost. Idling at the gate, they are twenty minutes early, a perfect cushion time-wise to scope out the school and the scene.

Trina nods at the BMW. "Nice ride."

"You'll be seeing a lot of nice rides up here," Katie says.

"That's what you hear."

Trina sniffs, pulls down the passenger-side visor, and peers at herself in the mirror on the flap. By reflex, she begins to apply a fresh coat of lipstick. Katie shakes her head.

"What?" Trina says. "I'm at Pemberley. I must beautify."

"Please," Katie says.

They are jolted by the medieval moan of the gates opening. The BMW drives through, then the gates jerk closed. Katie pulls forward and announces their names into the call box. After a moment, a metallic genderless voice echoes into their car, "Welcome to Pemberley," and the gates grind open.

Katie follows the taillights of the Beemer past a wide, steep set of stairs leading up to the Pemberley campus and into a concrete parking structure. Katie's SUV is fifth in line, behind the BMW, a black Mercedes 600SL, a forest green Jaguar, and a Mercedes SUV.

"It's official," Trina says. "We have the worst car here."

"By far," says Katie.

"If the parking lot is any indication, these are not my people."

"You can't hate the school because of the cars in the parking lot," Katie says.

"Yes I can. And I do. I'm not applying here. Let's go home."

"Shut up. I want to see it."

"Why? You want Alex to do four hours of homework a night in kindergarten? This is not your school. Your school is Hunsford."

"And your school is?"

Trina shrugs. "Still looking. I'll know it when I see it."

Katie drums her fingertips on the steering wheel. "You have nothing to worry about. You'll get in everywhere."

"You talking about the *D* card, girl? You bet I'll be waving it."

"Ah, to be young, single, and Mexican."

"Half," corrects Trina. "But it's enough. Hopefully."

"Christ. How long does it take Beemer Boy to park?"

The BMW slithers into a narrow spot between a wall and yet another Mercedes. Katie's SUV inches forward.

"Pay dirt," Trina says. She points to an opening next to a silver Lexus.

"Probably the janitor's car," Katie says.

"I'm not gonna like this place," Trina says.

"At least you have a positive attitude," Katie says.

•   •   •

Trina D'Angelo, born Katrina Manuela Jimenez, has café mocha skin, high, sculpted cheekbones, a model's height, an athlete's build, and a DJ's voice. Her eyes are bullet brown and penetrating, her laugh booming and intimidating. Married briefly to a drummer in a grunge band, Trina bolted when her living room started to look and smell like the bowl of an oversized hash pipe. She left the marriage feeling nauseous, which she attributed to the sickness of the union itself. Two weeks later, she discovered that her nausea was actually due to morning sickness. She called her husband with the news and offered to reconcile for the sake of their unborn child. He acknowledged her pregnancy with a drunken grunt and reacted to her suggestion that they get back together by hanging up the phone.

That was five years ago. Today, to Trina's surprise, her ex plays a part in Pascal's life—granted, a small part, but it seems to be enough for their son. It's certainly more than enough for Trina. The ex calls Pascal on weekends and holidays, occasionally pops in for a visit, and even more occasionally mails Trina a support check. Not exactly the perfect father, Trina admits, but better than some. In any case, she and Pascal are doing fine without him or any other man. Trina takes some credit for her ex's turnaround. Heeding her advice, a year ago he ditched the band and partnered into a national muffler and brake franchise in Philadelphia. The ex seems, if not entirely happy, relatively coherent.

Trina was born in Mexico City to a Mexican barber and a Caucasian medical student, a liaison that Trina never understood. Her parents did manage to stay married for six years, five and a half of them in New Jersey where her mother gave up studying medicine and her father gave up her mother. Living in Mexico for a grand total of six months scarcely qualifies Trina as Mexican, but it is technically true. As her best friend Katie Miller says, "Trina, you're as white as I am."

"Whiter," corrects Trina. "But when it comes to getting into kindergarten, *yo* am Mexican."

"*Yo* don't even speak Spanish."

"Not true. Oh, Pascal, honey! Mamacita's right here! Where is my *niño?*"

Katie just laughs. In truth, it has been a struggle for Trina. Her finances are tight. She works as a caterer out of her home, a spotty career at best, though it seems to be picking up. Late at night, after Pascal is asleep, Trina tinkers at a portable keyboard and dreams of becoming a singer-songwriter like her idol, Lucinda Williams.

"I have so many songs in my head," Trina says. "Someday I'm going to write a song about this whole crazy kindergarten application process. I bet that would sell."

• • •

The Pemberley School campus lies nestled in what appears to be an arboretum, wide as Central Park, green as a golf course. The school's vine-covered stone buildings—administration, classrooms, and library to the right; auditorium, gymnasium, art room, and science lab on the left—horseshoe around acres of a lush lawn large enough for a soccer match. You might compare Pemberley to a smaller version of Oxford University.

Slightly out of breath, Katie and Trina complete their ascent up the thirty-seven concrete steps from the Pemberley School parking structure onto the school's grounds. They stop, riveted, taking in the scene before them: three hundred prospective parents munching hors d'oeuvres, conspiring in hushed tones, sharing information and anxiety, laughing nervously. These parents are dressed to the hilt, men and women in black suits and cocktail dresses, seriously moneyed, card-carrying members of the ruling class, distinguishable only by paper nametags with squiggly blue borders pressed close to their hearts.

"This is, wow," says Katie.

"Holy shit," says Trina.

"Hi!"

A baby-faced African-American boy wearing a red Pemberley blazer and short blue pants extends a puffy hand toward Katie and Trina.

"Welcome to Pemberley. I'm Simon. Please sign in over there at table number three, fill out a nametag, and enjoy some refreshments before you go into the information session, which will be in about fifteen minutes. And if you have any questions about Pemberley, don't hesitate to ask. I've been here for five years."

Trina bends down to him. "Hey, Simon, how old are you?"

"Ten."

"You like this place?"

"Oh yes. I love going to school here."

"What do you like about it?" Katie asks.

"Hm. Let's see. Well." Simon presses a finger to his mouth. "I guess I like everything. I like the kids and the teachers. Yeah. I like everything."

"What don't you like about it?" Trina asks.

"Hmm." Finger again to his lip. "I wish school started later. And it was only four days a week. I like to sleep in sometimes and do nothing all day except play video games."

"That's interesting," Trina says, and Simon beams.

"Well, thanks," Katie says.

"See you around," Trina says.

"Do you need help finding the sign-up table?"

"Nope. We got it," Trina says.

"Welcome to Pemberley," Simon says as he greets a couple dressed in matching black gabardine suits despite the warm evening. Katie and Trina move toward the center of the courtyard.

"Look at these people," Trina says. "I feel like I'm in Stepford."

"Ask yourself. Can you see Pascal running around, playing soccer on that field?"

"Actually," Trina says, "I can."

•   •   •

Moments later, officially signed in, nametags slapped on, hands balancing plastic plates punctuated with fresh fruit, Wheat Thins, and slices of aged sharp cheddar, Katie and Trina stand on the periphery of the courtyard observing the swirl of humanity ten feet away.

"These people seem so, I don't know, desperate," says Katie.

"Yeah, but the fruit is incredible," Trina says. "And this cheese is killer."

"You never had cheese before? You have cheese every time you come to my house."

"Not like this cheese. This is Pemberley cheese."

Katie scans a cluster of parents to her right, then glances at another group next to them. "Unbelievable. Everybody's staring at each other's nametags. They're trying to see if someone more important than they are is trying to get their kid in."

"I know. It's disgusting," Trina says. "Did you see whatshername over there?"

"Who?"

"The TV weather lady."

Katie cranes her neck at Trina. "You're looking at nametags too."

Trina shrugs and pops a slice of kiwi into her mouth. "I heard that her kid is totally off-the-wall and obnoxious, unlike Pascal, who is intelligent, athletic, charming, and, have I mentioned, Mexican?"

Katie rolls her eyes. "You are such a nut job. Why am I friends with you?"

Trina lays her plate down on one of the six food stations, picks up a napkin and presses it lightly to her mouth. Then she slips her arm into Katie's and pulls her toward the Pemberley School auditorium.

"Come on, honey, let me show you around Pascal's new school."

• • •

The auditorium at Pemberley rakes upward at a sharp angle, providing a perfect sight line from every seat. The seats themselves are made of cushy maroon velvet, and the rows are wide enough for a six-footer to stretch out in. The sound system, newly installed a year ago, is voice-activated, adjusted automatically for clarity rather than volume. A dozen lighting instruments hang suspended from a ceiling grid like a swarm of black metal moths.

Dana Optt stands in the funnel of the auditorium, in front of the stage, bathed in soft blue light. She wears a sky blue suit in perfect balance with her background. She raises her hand and the three hundred prospective parents seated before her instantly silence themselves.

Dana ducks her head in response, an awkward, almost shy gesture, her exquisite white coif waving slightly. After eleven years as director of admissions at Pemberley, she still can't get used to the deference a crowd like this showers on her. She knows also that this deference is short-term, lasting for only a few intense months, and that she is viewed most often as both a messenger of hope and the deliverer of heartbreak.

For Dana, the best part of her job is being around children. "I love the kids," she says. "Why else would you work in a school? In fact, the one bad part of my job is that it's very isolating. So I go out of my way to find time to hang out with the kids. I eat lunch with them. I do carpool. Yeah, I'm crazy about the kids."

Dana takes one step to the side, and behind her on a screen covering the entire back wall, faces of children appear in the blue light: a six-year-old African-American girl wearing braces; an eleven-year-old Asian boy laughing hysterically, his arms spread around two classmates; a white girl missing two front teeth; and a lanky Hispanic student wearing Pemberley red. The PowerPoint presentation continues with a barrage of laughing, happy children of all colors, races, and creeds. Underscoring the photos, soft rock sells the happiness even harder. The presentation ends with two children pointing right at the audience, one black, one white, two fingers up on each of their little hands, waving the peace sign.

"Those are the faces of Pemberley," Dana says. She stands now at a podium, which during the PowerPoint presentation has arisen out of the stage floor.

"Do you know what I love about kindergarten?" Dana asks the crowd before her. "Everything is still possible."

Dana pauses for a tiny beat to allow the three hundred–plus parents before her to absorb this simple, pithy thought. "That is the Pemberley philosophy. We hold on to that for as long as possible. We want children to keep these three words in their heads and their hearts forever: *Yes, I can!*"

If Dana could observe the three hundred faces in the crowd in close-up, she would see a hundred heads nodding fervently, accompanied by a dozen women actually tearing up.

"I know this is the beginning of what will be a year of stress and anxiety and, inevitably, disappointment. But I want to say one more thing to you, as a parent and as an educator."

Again, Dana pauses. Her voice, amplified through the crystal-clear acoustics in the auditorium, is melodic and full of weight. "Don't rush. Enjoy your last year of preschool. It's precious time. Don't waste it. Don't lose it. And don't prep your kids for kindergarten. Please. Don't drill them with flash cards. Don't put them in intensive, inappropriate math programs. Don't . . . do *not* coach them for their school visits. Please. I know it's hard, but try to *relax.*"

A huge laugh.

"I mean it. If for no other reason than your child will pick up on your anxiety and will feel anxious herself. And she won't know why. And what are you going to tell her? You can't tell her anything. You shouldn't. You'd better not. I wish we—and I do mean we, because I'm right in the middle of it—could just allow our children to *be*."

Applause.

"I want to say a few words about Pemberley and then I'll give you some cold, hard facts. The best way to describe Pemberley is that we are academically challenging and developmentally appropriate. Our key word here in all things is *balance*. We teach the basics, reading, writing, math, science, the arts, and we teach kids how to cooperate with each other. We have small classes and we divide these small classes further into small groups. We want our kids to learn how to collaborate. One of the differences between us and public school is that we get to choose our own curriculum. We get to tailor what we teach to our own population."

A hundred pens scratching paper, scribbling notes, clicking like a field of crickets.

"You will hear all about our curriculum in more detail when you take the tour. But to sum it up, our goals at Pemberley are to teach children confidence, independence, and how to learn. Now. Let me just bust one myth. The Pemberley Homework Myth. The number one question I'm asked? 'Mrs. Optt, is it true that the kids at Pemberley have four hours of homework a night?'"

Dead silence.

"Okay, here's the truth. You ready? In kindergarten, there is no homework. In first and second grades, the kids have a total of thirty minutes a night—twenty minutes of reading, and ten minutes of other subjects. In third grade, kids have to read a half hour a night, and they have another twenty minutes of homework. Fourth grade, it goes up to forty-five minutes a night, in fifth grade it's an hour. By sixth grade, which is middle school, kids get between sixty minutes and ninety minutes a night. That's it. That's the truth. Four hours a night in kindergarten? Until fifth grade, they don't have four hours a *week*."

A hum buzzes through the crowd.

"I don't know how these rumors start, but now you have the facts. And if you don't believe me, ask any of the student senators who are with us tonight. They'll set you straight."

She nods at a group of students seated together in the front row. One of them says something to her. She cups her fingers over her ear. "What, Simon? You don't have any homework?"

Simon, the boy who greeted Katie and Trina, leans over two other children and speaks inaudibly to Dana.

"Oh," Dana says. "You don't *do* any homework."

The audience laughs. Dana grins at Simon. "Simon is our resident comedian." She glances back at Simon, who bobs his head in agreement.

"Now, I know you're all wondering," Dana says, "what kind of child are we looking for? I am looking for all kinds of kids. We don't want a class of just extremely bright, high-achieving kids. We want a mix. We want kids who are loud and energetic and kids who are shy and laid-back. We want kids who are leaders and ones who will grow into being leaders. A well-balanced group. That's what we're looking for. Now, what about getting into Pemberley? What do the numbers look like for next September? Well, look around. There are over three hundred of you here tonight and this is only our first of six open houses. My math is rusty but I think that's eighteen hundred people coming through here. Of course, not everyone will submit an application. But that's why you're here: to see if Pemberley feels right for you, for your child, and for your whole family. We are not a drop-off school. If that's what you want, you're in the wrong place. We are a community. And we want you to make a commitment to become a part of our community. If this all sounds right to you, then follow me, and let's tour the campus."

The hum returns. Only now it builds to a crescendo resembling the opening musical sting in an action movie, signaling that the first bloody battle is about to begin.

• • •

Camped on the left side of the auditorium, two-thirds of the way up, Trina D'Angelo turns to Katie Miller.

"Oh. My. God," Trina says. "I love her."

"So you want to stay?" Katie suddenly sounds winded.

"You don't want to take the tour?"

"I don't know. I'm tired. Do you like it?"

"For Pascal, yes. For me, no. I mean, I drive a Honda."

"Miles could never relate to these people. Alex would be fine. Alex will be fine anywhere. Alex would be fine in public—"

Katie stops in midsentence. She realizes that she and Trina are the only two people left in their section.

"It's kind of now or never," Trina says.

Katie doesn't move.

"You know what," Trina says quietly. "Let's go. I've seen enough."

"But you like it—"

"I like the school. I like what Dana said. Everybody's telling me Pascal would love it here. But look around. I'm not fitting in with these parents. Plus I'm never getting in."

"What about the *D* word?"

"I don't think my kind of diversity works here. That Simon kid is probably Condi and Colin's secret love child."

"Aw, screw it." Katie is on her feet, sidestepping out of the row. "Let's take the tour. It's more information. Come *on*."

Trina sighs, gets up. "You're driving me crazy, you know that?"

CHAPTER FOUR

A Thick Folder, a Thin Applicant

When it comes to the applications, it's amazing. Half of the parents can't write and the other half are clueless.

—*an educational consultant*

The Application

What should I write on the application to make me—I mean, my child—stand out?

Step One.

Call the schools you're applying to and have them send you an application.

This is not as easy as it sounds.

Some schools refuse to send you an application. In order to *maybe* receive an application from these schools, you must first enter a lottery. You do so by *pre*-applying, filling out a postcard prior to a certain cutoff date. A few weeks later, someone, presumably the director of admissions, will draw a hundred postcards out of, I imagine, a bin or tumbler similar to those on a game show or, as in dreaded days past, the draft lottery. The school then mails applications to those lucky one hundred, to be returned within the month, filled out and accompanied by a $125 check.

61

Another school invited an unlimited number of applications to be submitted, but when it came time to schedule tours and interviews, the admissions director allegedly pulled seventy-five applications for girls out of a hat and seventy-five applications for boys out of another hat.

"I actually saw the hats," an educational consultant told me. "The boys' hat was a baseball cap and the girls' hat was a straw hat. I found it interesting, though, that when the one hundred and fifty applicants were pulled out, somehow the most prominent families in the city were magically chosen. I've heard they've since abandoned the hats but they still only take a hundred and fifty applications. How they choose them is anyone's guess."

I encountered the most exclusionary method of parceling out applications when I visited an elite school in an expensive suburb of a major city. I politely asked the receptionist for an application. She told me that I had to go home, call back, and request a tour and an interview with the director of admissions, who, after spending an hour with me and my wife, would determine at that time if she would allow us to apply.

"So you actually prescreen all your prospective parents?" I had to repeat this because I wasn't sure I understood.

"Yes. We find it a very efficient weeding-out process."

Rumors abound. Some schools, the Evergreen School among them, supposedly consider only the first one hundred applications they receive. Of course, they don't necessarily notify you if your application does not fall within the cutoff. Other schools, including Meryton, allow you to tour the school only after you have submitted your application and paid your $150 application fee, after you've "won" their lottery.

"That place is shrouded in mystery," Katie Miller said. "Since they don't let you see it until you apply, you have to go solely by what you read in their brochure or what you hear around. So when it says on the application, 'Tell me how your family values match the philosophy of the school,' you're kind of strapped. You have to write something right out of their mission statement. What else can you do? It's very frustrating."

      •   •   •

Step Two.

    Fill out the application.

    Your mission is to hook the reader while not raising any red flags.

Application for Admission
Kindergarten
A TOP-TIER PRIVATE SCHOOL

Sibling Due Date: SEPTEMBER 10
General Due Date: OCTOBER 15

The Early Bird Special

After narrowing her school choices to five, Katie Miller put herself on the clock and laid out a schedule that drove her to complete all of her applications by the last week in August, in plenty of time for her husband to go over them, make his notes and edits, and for her to get them in to the schools during the first week of September, well ahead of the October 15 deadline.

"A friend of mine told me to get the applications in early if you really want a school, because even if they don't say it, schools look at the first applications more seriously. I'm taking her advice. For one thing, I want them out of my life; want them off my plate, onto their plate. But it is partly calculated as to when they get them. I want to appear serious. I don't know if it makes a darn bit of difference."

New York mom Shea Cohen also used the summer to complete all seven of her applications, including writing the general essay required by six of the schools. She printed out her first draft and gave it to her husband, Donald, for a once-over. He went through it methodically with a red pencil. Shea incorporated his changes and finished the applications by the second week of August.

"Mission accomplished," Shea said with a massive sigh.

Trina D'Angelo and Lauren Pernice waited until the eleventh hour to finish their applications. Trina put off writing hers because she was "frozen."

"I hate this," she told Katie. "It's gross. I don't know what to write. I'm only applying to three schools. Will you write them for me? Please? Don't forget to mention that I'm Mexican."

Somehow Trina managed to complete the three applications herself, mailing them a few days before the due date.

"Are you going to drive them over?" Katie asked her.

"Katie, unless the deadline is like *today*, you do not hand-deliver your applications. That makes you look so desperate."

"We are desperate."

"I know, but we don't want to *look* desperate."

Lauren applied to only two schools—Pemberley, truthfully her first and only choice, and Wickham, a late entry.

"We added Wickham because it seems, I don't know, *insane* to apply to just one school," she said, her Virginia lilt accenting the apparent absurdity of her decision. "We threw in Wickham because (a) it's got a good reputation, but when we visited we thought it was so homogenous and bordering on the militaristic that it didn't really speak to us, and (b) it is geographically desirable, as in, five minutes from our house in traffic. So it's just Pemberley, please God, and Wickham, ridiculously, our backup."

Lauren typed out her applications and presented them to her husband, Craig. He pored laboriously over what she'd written.

"No, no, no," he said, crossing everything out. "This doesn't tell you anything. We have to start over."

Craig and Lauren then sat down together and rewrote the applications side by side, with Lauren providing much of the content and Craig supplying the style. In total, Lauren estimates that they spent between six and eight hours on the applications. They finished the morning of October 15. Craig dropped off the Wickham application on his way to work and Lauren drove the application to Pemberley and hand-delivered it to Gail, Dana Optt's assistant.

Do Katie and Shea have an advantage because they submitted their applications earlier? Does their timing underline their seriousness or show a sense of desperation?

"Doesn't matter if you get your application in early or late," Dana Optt said. "Doesn't matter at all. It doesn't matter if it's sent by mail or dropped off in the office. I don't care if it's typed or handwritten. People ask me if I prefer laser or inkjet. It. Does. Not. Matter."

Applicant

BOY   GIRL *(please circle)*

FULL LEGAL NAME: Killian Michael Pernice

NAME STUDENT PREFERS (NICKNAME): Killian

DATE OF BIRTH: April 21, year

CURRENT SCHOOL: Bright Stars

FATHER'S EDUCATIONAL BACKGROUND: BA

COLLEGE AFFILIATION: Harvard

MOTHER'S EDUCATIONAL BACKGROUND: BA; MA

COLLEGE AFFILIATION: Harvard

Legacy

"Here is something important that we look for in the application."

MK, director of admissions at the Longbourne School, paused, then spoke barely above a whisper. "Legacy. That has a lot to do with getting into college. I look to see where the parents went to college. If they went to Princeton, Harvard, Yale, then the kid's got a good chance of going there as well. They're legacies. So if you're a K-through-twelve school, where the parents went to college matters. Nobody will admit it, but it's true. For good reason. You don't want parents who didn't go to a certain college thinking that they're at a disadvantage. But we look at it. Both parents went to Harvard? Kid's a double legacy. We like that. A lot."

The New Middle

Please send me a financial aid application.

With the cost of private school soaring, threatening to reach a stratospheric $30,000 per year, more families than ever before are considering applying for financial aid. But how do you know if you qualify? Is there a cutoff figure?

"There was a statistic that came out recently," said Dana Optt, Pemberley's director of admissions. "Right now, if you make $192,000 a year, you're eligible for financial aid. We call these people the New Middle."

If the New Middle makes what ten years ago would have defined them as upper-class, then we are witnessing an alarming downward spiral. The *Old* Middle has apparently plummeted into what is now lower-class, and our former lower-class has, by logic, sunk into poverty. The distance between the New Middle and the New Lower has widened, exponentially, frighteningly.

Red Flag #1: See Attached

From your perspective, in what kind of learning environment would your child thrive?

See attached.

What individual and family activities does your child enjoy?

See attached.

If your child is currently attending a nursery school or preschool program, please briefly describe the program and comment on your child's experience in that program.

See attached.

Tell us about your child's characteristics, traits, personality, and maturity so we may have a clear picture of how you view him or her. If your child has any special needs, please discuss them here.

See attached.

How would you as parents like to be involved in supporting the school community?

See attached.

Please feel free to include any additional comments about your child or your family.

See attached.

MK reflected the opinion of many school officials: "The one red flag that's consistent is length. I get so many applications that are ridiculously long. I honestly will not read them. I won't read the essay unless it's short and concise. I'm sure parents put in a lot of time and energy, but there's an old saying: 'The thicker the folder, the thinner the applicant.'"

Edgar Mantle, the head of Evergreen School, agreed.

"My number one red flag, by far, is *quantity*," he said. A large man, a former college basketball player whose width has started to catch up to his height, Edgar favors tweed sports jackets and colorful ties. He speaks operatically in both volume and gesture, reminding you of the late raconteur Peter Ustinov.

"We have a two-page application and not much room for people to write things," he said. "We do that on purpose. But there are people who still write on every line, 'See attached.' And they'll send a ten-page, single-spaced typewritten thing. To me, that sends a message. The message is they're always going to be in my office because everything is not going to be just so. And their child is *so* precious. 'Oh, they asked. They must really want to know all about him.' Yeah. I'd *love* to read ten pages about your kid."

Red Flag #2: Regurgitation

For what reasons would Hunsford School be a good fit for your family philosophically?

Hunsford's philosophy takes into consideration the uniqueness of each child. Alex is eager to learn. She took her first dance class this summer and emulated the teacher's every movement and wanted to learn. Further, Hunsford places a strong emphasis on academics while teaching in a very comfortable environment.

Katie Miller peeked over the top of the Hunsford application, and whispered, "I'm kind of quoting what they said in their . . . thing. Is that a no-no?"

"To me, the number one red flag is people who pull stuff right out of the catalog," an admissions director said. "Or right off the Web site. Word for word. What do they think, I'm not going to recognize it? People do it all the time, every year. Amazing. Blows my mind."

A school head added, "The point of the written application is to create talking points so when I'm in the interview I can refer to what the parents have written. I will key a couple of things that are important to me to bring up. I don't want people obsessing over what to write. And don't think, *What answer do they want?* It doesn't matter. I care about what you *value*. That's essentially it. I think that parents make choices as parents. And I think that the application tries to get at what kinds of choices are important to you. There really isn't a right or wrong answer. The application is just an opportunity for parents to express themselves a little bit so we can get to know the families in the interview. If what they say is right out of the brochure, I write that down. It's a red flag. I want the parents to be real."

Red Flag #3: Nut Jobs

What individual or family activities does your family enjoy?

Last summer, our family spent three weeks in Tibet following the Dalai Lama. The moment we began our inward and outward journey, Hannah and the Dalai Lama connected in some deep metaphysical way. They would communicate totally without speaking but it was clear to everyone in the ashram—and to the Dalai Lama himself— that Hannah is a child blessed with an old soul and that

perhaps she was a shaman in another life. She is certainly wise well beyond her four years.

"When a parent writes something that's nuts?" said MK, director of admissions at Longbourne in New York. "Big blinking red flag."

"Normally people are very guarded in writing their applications," Brianna, director of admissions at the Hunsford School, said. "Often the applications are only marginally related to the people who write them because so many people are taking notes on the tours, writing down buzzwords they hear that they send back to us on the applications. You get a lot of that. When someone goes way over the top, it's easy to spot."

Dana Optt at Pemberley said, "To me, one of the most important questions is, 'What individual or family activities does your family enjoy?' I'm really looking to learn about the family. Tell me about family trips, taking bike rides, that sort of thing. You don't have to wow me. In fact, the more low-key, the better. Don't tell me that your family toured the Sistine Chapel last summer and little Johnny or little Mary had a spiritual awakening at the age of four. I'm not buying it. I'll bet they were bored to tears. Don't go nuts on the application. When in doubt, talk to your preschool director. Most of them are sophisticated about the process. They'll catch the stuff that's off-the-wall."

Occasionally, though, something falls through the cracks.

A few years ago, a family submitted an application to Pemberley in which the parents described their child in such an over-the-top way that Dana dreaded meeting them.

There's nothing left, Dana thought. *This kid has done everything. He's like the messiah or something.*

They didn't stop there. One morning Dana's assistant, Gail,

came into Dana's office. She was clearly trying to suppress a smile and failing.

"You just got a package," she said.

"Okay, bring it in," said Dana.

"I'd really like to but I can't. You're gonna have to come out into the hall."

Dana followed Gail out of her office. In the middle of the hallway stood a five-foot-high package swaddled in brown wrapping paper. Dana ripped off the paper and found herself staring at a huge picture of the messianic child from the application, a photograph that the parents had blown up and mounted into a giant, self-standing poster.

"Help me understand," Dana said after staring at the picture in stunned silence. "Why would anybody do this?"

"You should see the size of their wallets," Gail said, finally allowing her laugh to escape.

Dana whirled back into her office, called the parents, and told them to pick up their picture immediately. They arrived within the hour. Dana met them in the hallway. But instead of an obnoxious, haughty couple, she found two sheepish, deeply embarrassed, down-to-earth people.

"We are so humiliated," the mom said.

"I have to know. Did somebody here give you the idea to do this?" Dana asked.

"No," the dad said. "It was all our idea."

"We're feeling so much pressure that we wanted our child to stand out," the mom said. "We knew the minute you called that we'd made a serious mistake."

Dana was confused. The people standing before her in the hallway seemed totally unlike the people who appeared on the application. She actually liked these people. They were humble, awkward, nervous; they were *normal*. Later, she phoned their preschool and spoke to the director.

"Did you see their application?"

"No. Why?"

"I'm gonna fax it to you."

Dana then told her about the picture. The director was stunned. She knew this couple as model parents, ideal candidates for Pemberley. In the end, Dana dismissed the giant photograph as an aberration and admitted the child into Pemberley.

"They are the most amazing family," Dana said. "The process had freaked them out. The trick is to be able to separate the people who are acting crazy from the ones who are truly nuts."

Be a Person

"When you write your application, there are two things you can do," an educational consultant tells her clients. "Distinguish your child in some way and show your passion for the school, your dedication, and your intention to work hard. And do your homework. Pay attention to the culture of the school. How is it different from other schools? Think about that."

New Yorker Shea Cohen knew that she had to somehow distinguish her son Liam on her application. She found this a challenge.

"Liam takes art class. That's really it. He tried soccer, didn't like it. He hasn't really done that much. I mean, he's *four*," Shea said. "What's outstanding about him is his personality. He's so sweet, just a nice, *nice* kid. He's very caring. He always looks out for the other kids, always tries to include them, loves to share his stuff. If he gets a new toy, he can't wait to show it to his friends."

Shea also thought it was important to write about their family. "I think the schools want to know who you are. What is your parenting style? Are you the kind of family that has your kid running from activity to activity all the time? Is your kid one of those programmed kids who goes from soccer to karate to art class? Or are you people who do a lot of family activities? That's more who we are. So we talked about our family, and the types of things that we do together. Finally, we talked about how we viewed Liam as an academic. What we think his academic potential is. We talked about his intellectual curiosity. We talked a lot about his early reading. We couched it in terms of his being precocious. In other words, it wasn't like, 'Oh, our son read early, isn't that phenomenal?' Didn't do that. We put it in terms that it has given him something he loves. It has expanded his mind and his world. Because his ability to read has enabled him to ask lots of questions about the world around him, about the things he's reading. And it gives him more and more mental activity, which shows us that he really needs to be in a place where he's intellectually stimulated. Liam is not a kid who wants to run in the park all day. Overall, we were to the point and specific. We wanted to paint a picture of our kid. We wanted the schools to get to know him. The worst thing you can do, I think, is to use a lot of adjectives. Your kid ends up sounding like a cliché and not a person."

· · ·

Standing over the stove, stirring a box of rigatoni noodles into a steaming pot, Katie Miller prepares dinner for Alex and her two-year-old brother, Nick. When the pasta is finished, she will toss it in a bowl with butter and Parmesan cheese, the kids' favorite.

"The last thing I wanted was to get caught empty-handed and find out I'd missed the deadline. That's why I started way ahead of time. I'm glad I did because I've seen Hunsford twice and I'm going back and I've seen Evergreen once and I'm going back there. That's what the luxury of time gives you."

Katie stirs the pasta slowly, then lays her wooden spoon down on the counter, where it teeters near the edge.

"I know this is important, but I'm trying to be as chill as I can. Some people are losing sleep left and right. When we went on the Pemberley tour, there was something about being among those parents that didn't fit. I consider myself more relaxed and laid-back and I didn't feel that I could ever be relaxed and laid-back with them. I felt a lot of anxiety around me that night. It was cutthroat. Way too cutthroat for me. I do think the admissions directors try to minimize the trauma as much as they can. They want people to feel comfortable at their school, but let's be honest. We're trying to get in and they're looking for people to take. If there were a few more schools in this town, it wouldn't even be an issue."

Katie checks the timer. Less than a minute to go. She wipes her palms on her apron, then absently picks up the spoon.

"I wish I could just settle for our local public school. I wish I could. I was talking to somebody yesterday who said, 'But your local school is getting better.' That's not good enough. In the beginning, I was feeling guilty when I started looking at private schools. I tried. I was open. I went to my public school. I visited, took a tour, asked questions. I wanted to know what I was saying no to. I wanted to know what everybody was complaining about. My attitude was, why is everybody being so snooty? Then I went on the private school tours and I saw that the private schools are far superior. More than just the reading and writing. The kids are going to learn to read and write anywhere. That's not the issue. It's who is my child going to become at the end of these seven years, nine years, thirteen years? That's the issue. Who is my child?"

A sea of white foam bubbles up in the pasta water. "Well, at least the applications are in. I think I'm in pretty good shape. We'll see. We'll find out next March."

The timer goes off, a series of high-pitched staccato beeps, sounding the alarm.

CHAPTER FIVE

So Many Fabulous Families

The thing about interviews is you know you're not always going to get honest answers. You're going to get what they think you want to hear. It's a little bit like a blind date. You know that everybody's going to be on their best behavior.

—a private school director of admissions

Shrink Session

What are admissions directors looking for in the interview?

In two words: normal and nice.

"All schools are looking for someone who is going to bust her butt, work hard, and be present. Every school wants normal folks. Nobody wants an obnoxious parent who is going to make everyone's life miserable," a school official said.

Educational consultant Emily Glickman expanded on this. "What you have to do in the interview is present a picture of an easygoing, pleasant family who is going to fit in well with the community and not cause any waves. No school wants parents who fight with teachers, who are demanding, or who are always making appointments with the school head. They want to enroll manageable parents."

But how do admissions directors find out who's naughty and who's nice? Beyond taking the word of preschool directors, who may have their own agenda when it comes to placing as many of their parents in top schools as they can, or the recommendations of the applicant's friends, admissions directors have to rely on their observations and instincts during the interviews.

"It's a total shrink session," Dana Optt said. "I know people come in here and they are very stressed out. I try to look at the process from their perspective. Plus, I am representing Pemberley. I am the first line. What you are going to remember is how I made you feel. I will do damage to the school if I don't give you the time and attention you need. I want you to feel that I am interested in you, which I am, and that you have an absolutely fair shot of getting in. You have paid a hundred dollars. I owe you that. I want you to feel, 'Okay, they spent time with me, they spent time with my kid, they showed me the school, they answered all my questions, and they treated me with respect.' And when the interview is over, I ask myself, 'Was I really fair? Did I have the right perspective? Did I jump the gun? Did I read the body language wrong?' It's intense for you and for me."

For some admissions directors, the key to "normal" may lie in how much parents talk about themselves.

"I try to steer the interview toward the kid. That's what it's all about for me," an admissions director said. "I want to know about the child's personality, her quirks, likes, dislikes, strengths, weaknesses. Just talk about her."

Dana Optt, like many admissions directors, considers herself a keen observer of human behavior. "I study body language. I watch how the two of you relate to each other. Are you on the same page? Who dominates? Is she going to let him speak? Does he want to be here? I watch the whole display. I get it all, the soft push, the hard push, and of course the name-dropping. Are you gonna go there? Are you gonna get into Who We Know? Are you going to try to impress me? Or are you just going to stick with your kid? It's also how you talk about your kid. If you ask me about algebra in first grade and you express deep academic concerns, I will note that. If you go on and on about how incredible your kid is in T-ball, I'll write on my form, 'They're going to need specialized math and they believe their child is the next Barry Bonds.' We'll never make them happy. Cross 'em off."

.   .   .

"I really love the interviews."

Edgar Mantle, head of Evergreen School, leans across his desk. He balls both hands into fists and pushes himself to his feet. "I enjoy relating one-on-one with families. Chatting. I like that."

Edgar gallops to a three-tiered metal filing cabinet planted in the corner of his office. He yanks out a drawer, licks his fingers, and rustles through a row of manila folders. He stops three folders from the back.

"Aha," he says, and snaps at the folder with his middle finger as if flicking away a piece of lint. He licks his fingers again, pulls a single sheet of paper out of the folder, and peers at it.

"Here we are. This gives an idea of how it's done."

He returns to his desk, sits back down, and places the sheet of paper in front of him. He runs his palm down the page, smoothing it out as if it's wrinkled. "When I sit down in my interviews, I refuse to have a standard set of questions. I read the application carefully. I see what leaps off the page. I then write down a couple of ideas about what I want to get the parents to talk about. I want them to talk about themselves, their kid, philosophy of education, what they're looking for. I try to be folksy. There are a lot of times at the end of a talk I have with parents where they'll say, 'Isn't there going to be an interview?' I say, 'I think that's what we just had.' For me, it's a kind of *feel* process."

He taps the sheet on his desk. "Having said that, and recognizing that this process is far from a science, although I don't know if I would call it an art either . . ."

Edgar slides the piece of paper across his desk. Across the top in bold type is the heading **Evergreen School Form For Parents' Admissions Interview**. Tucked immediately below is a cluster of lines requesting: "Child's name," "Date of birth," "An only child?" "Sibs' name(s) and age(s)," "Who toured? Mom____Dad____," "Mother's name," "Dad's name," "Mom's work," "Dad's work," "Nursery school," and "Other schools they are considering." Below this are a few more lines for comments after: "Notes from current school," "Notes from application," "Notes from Evergreen visit," and "General comments."

Edgar scratches his head, then rakes his fingers through his hair. "Every application is graded," he says. "Each person who participates in the process—myself, the kindergarten teachers, admissions director—gives a number 1, a number 2, or a number 3. In our system, 3 is the best. When you're only giving people three choices, you also have minuses and pluses. We all grade each application. A straight 3, chances are, is going to get in. We start looking to shape the classes after that. We start looking beyond the 3s. Now, what makes a 3? For example."

Edgar nods at the fifth line on the page. "Nursery school. I look here and I might say, 'Oh, I've known so-and-so who's run this nursery school for years.' That's a good recommendation."

Edgar lifts his shoulders in a shrug massive enough to wriggle out of a winter coat.

"We then have five questions taken directly from the application, with a space for the number value. 'Parents' description of child on application.' Then 'How parents may participate,' and 'Previous school's description of child.' So each member of the committee gives a number there after reading the application. Then these bottom categories are notes from the interview. You want to ask questions that give you a sense of the parenting style, the family activities, and any other family information that's relevant."

The bottom of the form lists several questions in bold with a line preceding each question for the number value and an inch space beneath for comments. The questions are: "How do you see Evergreen? What similarities/differences between the schools you are applying to? How will you choose?" "Educational philosophy/past school experience: Do parents agree?" "Participation—How? What level?" and "Notes re child from interview."

"You're trying to get people to give you information," Edgar says. "The bottom line is, what kinds of things can you tell me besides what I read in the application?"

Edgar shakes his head. "We may be more thorough than we have to be. I don't know. I will say this: you don't need all 3s to get a 3. There's a place on the bottom of the form that says, 'What's your overall score and why?' So you might look over everything and say, 'I gave this person two 2s, but this is the best family I've met in a long time.' Like I said, this process is not scientific."

.   .   .

In every season there are stories:

Mr. Big

Mr. Big sat on the couch in the admissions director's office. He was well-known, a *player*, his face frequently grinning haughtily from the glossy city magazine's gossip pages, his wisdom often quoted in the business section of the paper. He was pushing seventy now and had recently married for the fourth time. This wife had just celebrated a traumatic birthday of her own, her thirtieth.

Mr. Big stretched his arm across the top of the couch. His long fleshy arm traveled nearly end to end. He smirked and puckered his lips as if he were puffing on an imaginary cigar. "Go ahead," he said.

"Go ahead and what?" the admissions director asked.

"Go ahead and start the interview."

"How do you think I should start?"

"Convince me that I want to be here."

The admissions director locked eyes with Mr. Big. "Actually, this is how it works. You need to convince me that I want you here."

Mr. Big instantly got smaller. Deflated. He withdrew his arm from the top of the couch and let it flop into his lap. "Oh," he said, as if he'd gotten the wind knocked out of him.

"Now, what we're gonna do," the admissions director said, "is focus on your child."

"I'm not used to this," Mr. Big muttered.

The admissions director knew what he meant but said anyway, "What?"

"Not being the one who decides."

The admissions director smiled. "It's only for a few months, just until March. If I call you next September, you won't have any idea who I am, nor will you care."

"You're a hundred percent right," Mr. Big said. "And I probably won't take your call."

Mr. Big didn't get in.

Father's Day

"When it comes to the interview, if I could relay one piece of advice it would be relax," said Brianna, director of admissions at Hunsford School. "People come in here who are so uptight. They're literally shaking. I know this process can be overwhelming, but you have to take a few deep breaths and just chill. I sometimes spend half the interview getting people to calm down. I try to connect. I know how much time and effort people put into writing their application. I truly appreciate that. But you have to relax."

A couple came in for their interview. They were in their mid-thirties and they were both extremely nervous. "Let's talk about your child," Brianna said.

"We said everything in the application," the dad said.

Brianna smiled thinly. She saw that the dad's hands were shaking. "I've read your application thoroughly," she said. "But hearing you talk about your child is really helpful. I want to hear you describe your child's personality. Or talk about how you chose your preschool. Anything you want."

The dad turned ghost white. He looked at his wife. She shrugged. The dad looked back at Brianna. "I don't know—"

"Okay. What did you do this weekend? Did you do anything with your daughter?"

He lit up. "Well, actually, we were at my parents' house. They live in this planned community. I thought it would be an ideal place to teach my daughter how to ride a bike. No cars. Very safe. Wide-open areas. So I got her a bike. Got her all dressed.

She was wearing these brand-new little red sneakers. She got on the bike and I'm holding the bike. I'm behind her and all of a sudden I let go, and she was riding the bike all by herself. I felt this tremendous sense of pride. I was overwhelmed. I started to cry, watching my daughter ride her bike—"

The dad's eyes began to well up. He swiped a tear away from his cheek.

You're coming to the school, Brianna thought. She knew that she had an abundance of girls, but she was determined to take this family. And she did. They currently have three kids at Hunsford.

"I like people who spend a lot of time with their kids," Brianna said. "That, to me, is a major piece of the puzzle."

Stay on Target

A couple walked into the admissions office. The wife was extremely attractive, late twenties, laden with expensive jewelry. The husband was older, dressed in a blue pinstriped suit, his fingernails freshly manicured. They sat together on the couch. Dana Optt began the interview. She spoke briefly about Pemberley, and then asked them about their child. The wife began speaking in a monotone about her son. At one point she gestured, revealing an enormous diamond bracelet dangling from her wrist. Dana's attention veered from what the wife was saying to the jewelry on her arm. The diamond had the mesmerizing effect of a hypnotist's pocket watch; Dana could not stop looking at it. She had never seen anything so dazzling. It was like the Hope Diamond or something. Try as she might, she could not stop staring at the bracelet.

Oh my God, Dana thought, *she's talking about her son and I'm not paying any attention to her. I've lost my focus.*

Suddenly, the husband reached over and slapped his wife across the face. "Stay on target," he said.

It happened so fast that Dana wasn't sure that it happened at all. She replayed the moment, tried to erase it, but no, it was there, indelible in her mind. It had happened. The husband had reached over and just . . . *wham*.

The rest of the interview dissolved into a blur. Dana ran through her questions as quickly as she could; she didn't know what else to do. As soon as the couple left, she called their preschool and told the director what the husband had done.

"Oh no," the preschool director said. "He didn't do that in the interview, did he? I coached him to keep that behavior under wraps."

Dana canceled the rest of the day's interviews, went home, and took a hot bath.

Job Interview

The night before the Pemberley interview, Lauren Pernice pores over their application as intensely and thoroughly as if she were studying for a final. Sitting at her grandmother's antique whitewashed pine desk in the corner of the bedroom, she jots down notes, making sure she can instantly recall the exact wording she used to describe Killian's likes and dislikes, appealing qualities, and challenging characteristics. She underlines key phrases she and Craig chose to relate meaningful family activities, their philosophy about education, and their feelings about Pemberley. Then, with *SportsCenter* humming in the background, she and Craig fire possible interview questions at each other. They take turns being Dana. They anticipate what she might ask. They try to stump each other, but they are both fast and prepared. Finally, after a half hour, they call off the prep. Craig turns the volume up on *SportsCenter* and Lauren walks into their closet. Hands on hips, she cocks her head and confirms aloud what she has been thinking all week.

"I'm gonna wear the khaki slacks and a blue button-down. Simple. Comfortable. Casual but not over the line. What do you think?"

"Good," Craig says.

"What about you?"

"I'm wearing a suit."

His choice surprises Lauren. Craig is not a suit guy. He wears a sports jacket, no tie, for even his most important power meetings.

"Really? A suit?"

"I've been thinking about it," Craig says. "This is kind of like a job interview. I think I should wear a suit."

Lauren smiles. Craig has been typically tight-lipped since Gail phoned two weeks ago with their interview time: four o'clock Monday, the last interview of the day. Lauren, of course, has thought of little else. She has *spoken* of little else, except for the previous weekend when she and Craig took off for two days for a much-needed mini-vacation.

"One rule," Craig had said. "We cannot talk about schools. You have to promise."

Lauren had hesitated. She wanted to strategize. She didn't want Dana to throw her any curves in the interview.

"I promise," she'd said, reluctantly.

"The weekend was wonderful," Lauren related later. "We did not talk about schools at all. We did not talk about anything that would stress us out. It was so relaxing. I so needed that."

Lauren sits back down at the desk, adjusts her wraparound

Calvin Klein frames, and scans the application one more time. Satisfied, she slips the form back inside its plain brown envelope and calls her friend Susan, who had her interview with Dana Friday. She and Susan have traded voice mails all weekend. This time Susan answers. Lauren gets up from the desk and eases into an overstuffed rocker with a floral design, far enough away from the TV so as not to disturb Craig, who has now finished *SportsCenter* and found *Desperate Housewives*, a show she would normally watch. Instead, she curls up in the rocker and asks Susan for details.

"It was fabulous," Susan says. "We ran over."

"Seriously?" Lauren nervously lassos the phone cord around her left hand.

"All we did was laugh."

"Wow. Sounds like you kind of had fun."

"We really did. The time flew. Dana is amazing. But this poor couple who went after us? After the interview you go on a tour with a parent volunteer. The tour takes about a half hour. While we were walking back toward Dana's office, we saw the other couple leaving, going to the parking lot. They couldn't have been with Dana for more than thirty minutes. They didn't look happy. So, yeah, I think it went really well."

"That's great," Lauren says. "I just hope we do all right."

"Oh, come on," Susan says. "You guys will be fine."

"I hope so." But Lauren notices that she has absently twisted the phone cord into something resembling a noose.

•   •   •

The moment they pull into the Pemberley parking lot, Lauren loses her grip. It begins with an ache that wells up in the pit of her stomach. An unfamiliar taste rises into her throat. She realizes suddenly what she is feeling.

Terror.

Pure terror.

She and Craig walk into the hallway outside Dana's office ten minutes early. Relieved, Lauren looks for a water fountain. Not seeing one, she is happy just to have a few moments to compose herself, but then Dana appears, her mountain of white hair looming above her, dazzling, unnatural, and unsettling. Dana extends her hand. "Great. You're here early. Come in and we'll get started."

Oh no, Lauren thinks. Dana's eyes bore into hers like lasers. *I feel like she has X-ray vision. It's like she can look right through me and see into my soul.*

Lauren and Craig take the couch. Lauren inches close to him. Sitting in the armchair opposite, Dana takes notice of this. Craig breaks the ice. "I don't know if you remember but we met at the Private School Expo at Darcy. We'd been looking at different schools and hadn't made up our minds where to apply until we spoke to you."

"I do remember," Dana says.

She begins talking, describing Pemberley, touting the school, selling it as if they'd never heard of it. She speaks for a good ten minutes, maybe more. She speaks about Pemberley with such intelligence and passion that Lauren feels there is no better school on earth.

After what seems like forever, Dana wraps up her sales pitch. She shifts her position in her chair and says, "Okay, tell me about Killian."

As they'd agreed in the car, this is Lauren's cue.

Except she freezes.

She had everything planned. She knew exactly what she was going to say. She'd studied the application, committed all of the words, phrases, descriptions to memory . . . but now she draws a complete and total blank.

Finally, she blurts, "He's a terrific kid."

She searches her memory. Nothing. Zero. She wants to talk about how smart he is, tell her that he is gifted in math, but . . . nothing. The silence lasts only a couple of seconds but to Lauren it feels like an hour.

And then she hears herself speaking. It is almost as if she were watching this scene in a movie. She is saying, "Well, Killian is very bright but what really stands out is that he's a nice kid. He doesn't have a malicious bone in his body. He's genuinely happy for other kids when they do well. He is other people's champion."

She gives an example how in preschool he was the special-activity child last week. She and Killian prepared an activity for his classmates to do and he would be their teacher for an hour.

"He was very excited about this," Lauren says. "He was incredibly helpful to all the other kids. He kept bringing their papers over to me and saying, 'Look what so-and-so did, isn't that great?' He was so encouraging. I was very proud that he was my son."

Lauren finishes with a sort of cleansing breath. *Somehow I got through that,* she thinks. She smiles at Dana, not for approval, but for a response.

There is none.

Dana shifts position in her chair again and Lauren sees for the first time that she is holding a form of some kind on her lap. But Dana doesn't move a muscle. Doesn't lift a finger.

That's when Lauren knows things are going south. She remembers that Susan told her that Dana was writing madly during their interview, taking notes, circling numbers on the form. Not to mention how they laughed and carried on the whole time.

Lauren feels her heart sinking. She closes her eyes for the briefest moment and reminds herself, *Breathe.*

Then Dana begins talking about Killian. Thankfully, Craig takes over. At one point, she hears herself say, her Virginia drawl grating in her head, "Killian is academically advanced but socially he might need a little extra help."

"Sounds like he's smart but he also needs organizational skills," Dana sums up. She nods gravely and describes a couple of kids at Pemberley. She could easily be describing Killian. "Kids like Killian need to learn how to think outside the box," she says. "They need to explore other areas. A structured place might stifle him. He needs to be nurtured, to have his intelligence acknowledged, because he's a kid who can figure out that there can likely be more than one way."

Lauren thinks, *This woman is so insightful and so kind and that makes it awful because I love this school and I am* bombing.

The interview ends abruptly. Dana rises and escorts Lauren and Craig into the hall, where they meet an exuberant Pemberley mom who proceeds to take the Pernices on a quickie tour. The woman is annoyingly perky so it's easy for Craig to engage her in a running dialogue. Lauren barely says a word. At one point the perky mom says, "You can ask me anything at all. I don't report back to Dana."

Yeah, right, Lauren thinks. *It's fairly obvious that you're a spy.*

The tour ends. Lauren and Craig return to the admissions office and say their good-byes to Gail and Dana. Lauren does the best she can to sound upbeat but inside she is devastated, on the verge of tears. Walking to the car, she says, "Well, how do you think that went?"

"About a nine out of ten," Craig says.

She stares at him. "What? Where do you get that? It went horribly. I was dull and nervous and our interaction with Dana was flat as a board. I think I just cost our child his education."

"I don't see it that way at all," Craig says. "I think she was really engaged. I thought we articulated a clear philosophy and she reinforced it. We were very honest about our kid and she was responsive. And she sold the school to us. She wouldn't have wasted time doing that if she weren't interested in us."

"There was no spark. I got no sign of interest at all."

"Lauren, it was her last interview of the day. We were number seven out of seven. She was tired. She wasn't in a 'let's have a party' mood."

"This has to be a gender thing. That's the only explanation. I mean, it's amazing. I think it was a total bust. You think it went well."

"Yeah. I'm optimistic."

"And I don't think we have a chance in hell."

Dressed to Kill

Sealed into the corner of the white wicker couch in the admissions office of Meryton School, Trina D'Angelo waits to be called for her interview. According to her Swatch, she has been waiting for just under eleven minutes. She picks up last month's *Cicada* magazine from the white wicker coffee table and begins leafing through it. Outside of Pier 1 Imports, Trina has never seen so much wicker in one place. Twin white wicker chairs flank an egg-shaped wicker table strewn with *Cicada*s and *Highlights*. A wicker love seat angles weirdly into a back wall. An annoying wicker lampshade dangles overhead, offering diffuse light and the promise of crashing onto the love seat at any moment. Trina sighs heavily, as if she's just received horrible news. She takes another peek at the Swatch. Twelve minutes now. God *damn*. This waiting is torture.

Then, suddenly, she feels the sweat.

It's this stupid hat, Trina thinks. *Why did I decide to wear this thing? Now I'm stuck with it. I can't take it off. I'll look like Don King in the rain.*

The sweat is no mere rivulet leaking under the brim of her brand-new purchase, a lime green straw sun hat, the perfect accessory to her slightly darker green sundress. The sweat is pouring onto her forehead, forming a freaking pond. She should bolt into the restroom to regroup but she has already been in there twice. The receptionist, that frosty twenty-five-year-old with the perfect skin, will probably report to Elizabeth Marx, Meryton's director of admissions, that her two o'clock kept running into the bathroom, probably to do a line of coke. Feeling the lake on her forehead, Trina considers that she should just stand up, make some excuse, and flee.

I've made a giant mistake applying here, she thinks. *First of all, I've made a giant mistake with this outfit. A hat? Nobody wears hats anymore. It's a good thing I didn't go for the gloves, too. That would have been the topper. I mean, who am I, fucking Eloise?*

Trina swipes her forehead with her hand and examines her sweat-soaked palm. Without thinking, she dries her hand across the couch cushion. She looks up and catches the receptionist's eye. Trained on her. Frowning.

"Are you all right?"

"I'm fine," Trina lies. "It's just kind of hot in here. With the wicker and all."

"Can I get you some water?"

The receptionist is up from her desk and out of the room before Trina can answer. Her forehead is *flooding.* This time, screw it, she wipes the sweat and presses her palm into a page of *Cicada.* The receptionist appears and hands Trina a bottle of Arrowhead.

"Thank you," Trina says, and in one motion chugs half the bottle. "I'm sorry."

"No worries," the receptionist says, back at her post, rewired to a headset, an eye on the flat screen in front of her.

"I'm not usually like this," Trina says.

The receptionist smiles. A reassuring smile. Part of her job, Trina knows. To be reassuring. And sympathetic. They probably asked her to smile as part of her job interview. *Give me your best reassuring smile. That's good. Now give me sympathetic. No, that was kind of condescending. Good. That's it. You're hired.*

Trina drains the bottle. She stifles another big sigh. "I'm really not," she says.

The receptionist looks up, squints. "Excuse me?"

"Like this. Nervous. I don't get this way. I don't have a lot of stress in my life. There used to be. But I got control of it. Made some good choices. Career and personal. Yeah. Pascal and I live a pretty stress-free existence, all things considered."

"That's good." That smile.

"Oh God," Trina says and buries her head in her hands.

Breathe, she says to herself. *Just take your time and breathe.* Trina closes her eyes and takes a slow cleansing breath, the way she learned in yoga. She exhales and begins to count . . . *one, two, three* . . . hold . . . *one two three* . . .

When she opens her eyes, the receptionist is staring at her. Her once reassuring smile has become a gape of alarm.

"Do you want to breathe into a paper bag?"

"I'm okay," Trina says softly. "I'm breathing okay."

"Are you sure?"

"Yes. Thank you." Trina closes her eyes. Breathes. Exhales slowly.

"You know what it is?" she says, her eyes still closed. "I feel so vulnerable. I'm sitting here, waiting for this interview, and

I'm thinking, why am I even here? Meryton doesn't accept *any- body*. I'm never gonna get in. You know? I mean, you *do* know. It's silly. I'm here for one of five spots and you have a thousand applicants. What the hell am I doing here? What is Elizabeth Marx going to see in me? That's what I'm thinking. And that's why I'm sweating."

Trina D'Angelo opens her eyes. Standing in front of her is Elizabeth Marx, a short, round woman in her fifties with graying hair, high cheekbones, and deeply set blue eyes. She wears a light green sundress and a matching straw hat, nearly identical to Trina's.

"Seems like we have the same good taste in hats," Elizabeth says. "I'm Elizabeth."

"Trina." Somehow, some way, she is on her feet, feeling light-headed but shaking hands with Elizabeth Marx.

"I'm a wreck," Trina says.

"You're gonna be fine," Elizabeth says.

Trina nods, on the verge of tears. Elizabeth Marx puts an arm around her as if Trina were her elderly grandmother or a mental patient and leads her down a hallway, into her office, which is yet another celebration of wicker.

Trina lands on Elizabeth's couch, takes another deep breath, and is jolted when Elizabeth sits down next to her. But then Elizabeth asks where she bought her hat and they are off and running. They go from talking about hats to talking about parenting books. Trina reads them religiously and she and Elizabeth discover that among her favorites are two Elizabeth endorses. Only then do they move on to Meryton, the school's philosophy, and their philosophy of life in general. Elizabeth mentions a couple of current parents who have put in a good word for Trina. Trina relays a story about how she and one of the moms met in a parenting class for single mothers. At this point it's as if Elizabeth and Trina are dear friends out for a drink.

When Elizabeth brings up Pascal, it's almost as if she is talking about a student who is already enrolled in Meryton. Trina wonders if this is merely a tactic, the way Elizabeth makes every prospective parent feel, when in fact there is no hope whatsoever of getting in. Trina can't be sure. She does feel as if Elizabeth genuinely likes her. To seal the deal, she tosses off a mention of her Mexican heritage.

"I know," Elizabeth says. "I actually read your application. I also like that you're not from the wealthiest neighborhood in town. We have enough elite of the elite."

"Oh, Pascal and I provide all kinds of diversity. Ethnic, economic, cultural. All wrapped up in one family."

"One-stop shopping."

They begin laughing, so loudly that they don't hear the soft knocking on the door. The door inches open and the receptionist pokes her head in.

"I'm sorry to interrupt, but your three o'clock is here."

"Thank you. I'll be another five minutes."

Fifteen minutes later, Elizabeth reluctantly wraps up the interview.

"I really have to go. I can't keep those poor people waiting any longer."

She stands. Trina scrambles to her feet.

"It was so lovely talking with you, Trina. I mean that."

"Same here. And I'm sorry I was such a basket case in the beginning."

"You were freaked out for no reason."

Elizabeth offers Trina a shy, almost conspiratorial pout, then spontaneously the two women hug. The brims of their straw hats mash into each other momentarily, then snap back into place when Elizabeth and Trina pull apart.

"I will definitely be in touch with Gracie at Bright Stars."

"Great."

Elizabeth grabs both of Trina's hands and holds them. "I want you to do me a favor, okay? Relax. Don't worry. Everything's going to be fine. *Okay?*"

Trina nods. "Okay."

• • •

The moment she gets into her car, Trina calls Katie on her cell. On Katie's hello, Trina screams into the phone.

"*Ahhhhh!*"

"What?"

"The Meryton interview. I killed."

"*What?*"

"It was amazing. Elizabeth Marx is in-fucking-credible. I *love* her. And you know what's even better? She loves me!"

"Are you kidding me?"

"I am not kidding you. She loves me!"

"Tell me. Tell me everything."

"I don't know what to say. The whole thing is a blur. I was so nervous. I was sweating and practically crying and then we talked and we hugged and—"

"You *hugged*?"

"Yes! We fucking hugged! I was in there for an hour and fifteen minutes."

"This is unbelievable. You are in!"

"I am *in*," Trina says. "She gave every indication."

"I told you. Did I not say that you would get in everywhere?"

"You did. But now I'm having like this wave of doubt. I

mean, Meryton? Do I belong there? Elizabeth probably just gives great interview. You know what? It's all up to what Gracie says. They don't even meet the kid. It's so weird. Probably a good thing. Pascal would probably blow it."

"But the interview went that well? You could really tell?"

"Oh yeah," Trina says. "You can tell. You'll see."

• • •

For Katie, applying to Meryton has always felt like a formality.

"I feel like it's a waste of a hundred bucks," Katie says. "I can't really afford to throw away a hundred dollars. But I guess I'm looking at the whole Meryton application process as practice for Hunsford."

In fact, Meryton has already put her off. After mailing in the application, Katie expected to receive a postcard acknowledging that they had received it. After waiting two and a half weeks and hearing nothing, she called the Meryton admissions office to find out if they'd gotten her packet. They never called back.

"Those rat bastards," Katie says to Trina on their Sunday morning power walk. "They can't even call me back?"

"Maybe the postcard got lost in the mail," Trina says, elbows up like wings, jabbing at the air with her fists.

"With our old mailman, a distinct possibility."

"The crack addict?"

"We've got a new guy. He comes every day without fail between three and six. But at least he comes every day. That's a big improvement."

On Monday, Katie receives a letter from Meryton assigning her a Wednesday 10 a.m. interview time.

"I wanted to push it off a week. Give us a chance to prep," she tells Trina. "I called them and the assistant said, 'You could really help me out by taking this time.' I figured what the hell. It's before Hunsford so this will be like our practice one.'"

The night before the Meryton interview, Katie picks out her clothes. She has planned a different outfit for each interview, something appropriate for each school.

"I've taken marketing classes and you learn that, say, when you're doing telemarketing and you hear somebody answer the phone with a southern drawl, it might not be such a bad idea to start talking with a southern accent yourself. Because people feel they can relate to something familiar. For Hunsford, Brianna wears smocks. I don't really have anything like that, but the other women I've seen around her all tend to wear black sweater sets. So I'm pulling out my black sweater set for Hunsford. For Evergreen, Connie wears button-down blouses a lot. I have a button-down shirt all set for that interview. For Meryton tomorrow? Still haven't figured that one out. I heard that Elizabeth wears a suit usually, but she crossed me up with that whole sundress thing. I'm not wearing a suit. And I'm not showing up in a sundress and hat like Trina. I don't know. I go back and forth. Now, Miles wears the same thing every day, a pair of chinos and a T-shirt. Since it's the fall, he can wear a button-down shirt, chinos, and shoes, not sneakers. He's not wearing a suit or anything like that.'"

Katie goes to bed the night before the Meryton interview with only a vague idea of what she is going to wear. This lack of a specific plan is unlike her, but in the case of Meryton, her test case, she is willing to play it by ear.

In the morning, Katie is, as she says, "put together" in a white blouse, black pants, black shoes, and a little scarf, just because there's a bit of a morning chill. She stands at the counter in the kitchen taking one last hit of coffee when Miles comes in wearing chinos and a white T-shirt.

"What are you doing? What is that?"

"What?"

"You can't wear that. You have to wear a button-down shirt."

"Why?"

Katie throws her hands up in the air and rolls her eyes at an invisible person standing next to Miles. "You don't get it, do you?"

"Katie, I'm not trying to impress anybody."

"It's not that you're trying to impress them. It's just that you want to look like you're a presentable"—she struggles to match the right phrase with her rising anger, fails—"upstanding citizen."

Miles shrugs. "Bruce Springsteen doesn't wear a button-down shirt."

Katie stares at him. She blinks once, then speaks in the same slow, overly patient tone she uses with Alex when she is out of her head exasperated. "You know what? You're not Bruce Springsteen. You don't have that luxury. We're just regular people who want to show that we're respectful here."

She storms out of the room. Miles waits until she is out of sight, then mutters, "Really looking forward to the fight we're gonna have before Hunsford."

He rinses out her coffee cup, stacks it in the dishwasher, then goes upstairs to change.

•   •   •

They drive to Meryton in separate cars, Miles in the Volvo, Katie in the SUV. Right after the interview, Miles will leave for work and Katie will pick up Alex at Bright Stars and probably take her out to lunch. She has begun to prime Alex for her upcoming interviews. She is trying subtly to steer her in the direction of Hunsford.

"Daddy and I are going to visit a school today," she explained to Alex at breakfast.

"Which one?"

"It's called Meryton. We've heard it's very nice but we're not sure. That's why we're going there today. We want to talk to them and find out. But there's another school called Hunsford that I really like. I've visited there three times. The kids seemed so nice. They have a great playground, and oh, listen to this, Alex. They have a bunny. A pet bunny. Wouldn't you like to go to a school that has their own bunny?"

Alex shrugs.

"I wish I could've gone to a school like that," Katie says, turning to wipe off the counter with a clump of paper towel. Alex eyes her mother suspiciously.

·   ·   ·

"The hardest part of my job," Elizabeth Marx says as Katie and Miles settle into the wicker couch in her office and she pulls up a chair across from them, "is that there are so many fabulous families and so few spots."

Well, so that's it, Miles thinks. *Should I just get up right now, say, 'Nice meeting you,' and get the hell out of here? Because we're not getting in here. She just told us that.*

Instead, he nods in mock sympathy. Elizabeth smiles and opens a blue folder she holds on her lap. She is wearing a black-and-white blouse and dark slacks, not unlike Katie's outfit. She leans forward in her chair.

"Let's start by talking about Alex," she says, looking inside the folder. "I want you each to give me three adjectives that describe her."

Katie frowns. She wasn't prepared for a word association test to start off the interview. She searches her memory, tries to call up three words she used on the application. She hears herself say, "Charismatic, expressive, and charming."

"Energetic, cool, and hungry," Miles says. "And when I say hungry, I don't mean about food. I mean about life. She has this insatiable curiosity."

"Let's talk about that," Elizabeth says and, tilting her head toward Katie, warns, "and I want to know why you said 'charismatic.'"

For the next ten minutes they discuss Alex, elaborating on the words they chose. To Katie's surprise and, frankly, delight, Miles does most of the talking. When Elizabeth asks, "What are your biggest challenges with Alex?" Miles jumps right in.

"She can be very persistent if she doesn't get her way. She doesn't give up if you tell her no. She's going to try another tactic. She can be tough that way. Also, because she is so verbal, we can forget sometimes that she's only four. She will express herself so articulately that in a weird way it can be a problem on occasion. We want to challenge her and not be disrespectful of who she is as a person, but she is still only four."

"I get it," Elizabeth Marx says, nodding enthusiastically and writing something down on a form inside the folder. Then she asks, "What kinds of things do you guys do as a family?"

It clicks in then for Katie that Elizabeth is asking them a standard set of questions. She is not really engaging them in conversation; she is going through the motions, ironically, just the way Katie is.

"You could tell that we weren't really contenders," Katie says later. "It was kind of formal, kind of rote. Maybe if we had come in there bursting, saying, 'We just want you to know before we start that Meryton is our first choice,' it would have been a different type of interview. But we didn't. It was what it was."

Forty minutes in, after asking a few more questions about Alex, mainly in connection with her current school experience, Elizabeth closes the folder. Katie expects her now to get personal, to ask about them, their interests, their jobs, try to get to know them a little bit. Instead, she asks, "Do you have any questions for me?"

"I actually did prepare a few questions," Katie says, stuffing her hand into her purse and quickly retrieving her notebook.

"I also wrote down a couple of anecdotes and a few little notes about Alex," Katie says afterward, on the way to the car. "I wanted it all down on paper because, quite frankly, sometimes I choke. Sometimes my mind goes blank. I was thrown off by how formal Elizabeth was, so by the book. She was nice and all but . . . I don't know."

Katie scans the questions she wrote under the heading *Meryton*. She decides to go for question number three.

"Everybody talks so positively about Meryton. You have such a great reputation. Do you ever get complaints? What don't people like?"

"Lice."

Elizabeth holds for a moment, than laughs.

"That was a joke. Every school has lice. I'm sure Bright Stars—"

"Oh yes, we went through that as well," Katie assures her.

"Okay, let's see. Complaints. Well. I would say getting enough diversity. We are considered an elite school. We have no problem attracting families of means, people who can afford the tuition and more, but we're always trying to expand, to be inclusive of all sorts of people. That is a constant goal for us."

She taps her bottom lip with her index finger.

"And, okay, there is that element of Kate Spade versus Prada. There is always the kid who has one cashmere sweater who is trying desperately to be accepted into a circle of kids who each have forty cashmere sweaters. There is that."

Elizabeth Marx tilts her head again. "Did I answer your question?"

"Yes," Katie says. "Yes, you did."

Elizabeth uncrosses her legs, slaps the folder against her chair, and stands. "Unfortunately, I have to wrap it up."

Katie glances at her watch. The interview has taken forty-three minutes.

•　　•　　•

As Katie and Miles walk across the Meryton soccer field on the way to the parking lot, Katie whips off her scarf and jams it into her purse.

"That was what," Miles says, "a seven out of ten?"

"Yeah. Maybe," Katie says. They walk silently for a few seconds. "You were good, though. I was really impressed."

"Thanks. So were you."

"We're a good team."

She reaches over, takes his hand. Clasps it between both of hers.

"It's a long shot," he says.

"The longest shot. Our only chance is if the pool this year is full of really lousy rich famous people. If that happens and they have to go into the pool of regular people, then we have a chance."

"Could we have done anything differently in there?"

"Nah. And the more I think about her Kate Spade/Prada remark, the more disgusted I get."

They arrive at the parking lot. They stop, prepared to separate for the day. Katie gives Miles a coy smile.

"So, I guess, at the end of the day, it wouldn't have mattered if you wore a T-shirt."

She squeezes his hand and kisses him good-bye.

Very Strong Candidates

The night before the Hunsford interview, Katie insists that Miles look over the application. He takes the extra copy Katie made, sits up in bed with it, and begins to read it over. As he scans the first page, he says, "I think you're way over the top about this process."

"You call it over the top, I call it being thorough," Katie says from inside the closet. In a moment she appears wearing tan pants and her black cashmere sweater. "This is what I'm wearing tomorrow. You approve?"

Miles peeks over the top of the application. "You can't wear tan pants tomorrow. I'm wearing tan pants. We can't wear the same color pants."

Katie puts her hands on her hips and stares at her husband. "Are you giving me fashion tips? Are you out of your mind?"

"I was going to wear chinos."

"Not tomorrow you're not."

"I can't believe how you plan all this out."

"You know," Katie says, "we're not rich. I don't have this overflowing closet full of stuff. I only have a few outfits. I don't have a million things I can choose from."

"Fine," Miles says. "I'll wear something else."

"Not jeans, not a T-shirt, and not your dark wraparound sunglasses."

Miles shakes his head, continues reading the Hunsford application.

• • •

"I wasn't nervous, I was excited," Katie says. "The minute we walked into Brianna's office we felt very comfortable. Like we belonged there. I had good energy going the whole time."

Katie, Miles, and Brianna sit in chairs arranged in a semicircle. Brianna holds a manila folder on her lap. On top is another sheet. Katie can see a list of questions typed on it.

"Tell me about Alex," Brianna says. "Anything you think is important. I want you to talk about whatever you want. I have some questions"—she holds up the sheet for Katie and Miles to see—"and if I don't get the answers I need, I'll ask you."

"She is such a pleasure to talk to," Katie says. "Nothing about this felt like an interview. As opposed to Meryton, where Elizabeth had this list of questions and she just went down her list, boom, boom, boom, thank you very much, good-bye. It was the opposite of that."

This time, Katie begins. She starts by describing Alex as a good friend, someone who likes to nurture other kids. Within thirty seconds, she shifts the conversation to Hunsford itself and why the school is so perfect for their family, far and away their number one choice. Brianna smiles and nods and writes something on the question sheet. Throughout the interview she takes notes, but the conversation is always loose and informal. The feeling that Katie gets from the moment they sit down in Brianna's office is, *We want you to feel comfortable. We're not here to overwhelm you or frighten you.* To Katie, "It's a reflection of Hunsford as well."

Early on, Miles begins talking about his experience going to public schools. "There was no fostering of self-esteem at all," he says. "One of the reasons we like Hunsford so much is that you put such emphasis on developing a child's confidence. I had such a negative experience in high school especially, largely because I received no individual attention. I was uncomfortable speaking in front of the class and so forth. These are the things that Hunsford does. You help develop your students into good people."

Brianna nods. Smiles. Writes.

The interview flows easily. About ten minutes in, Katie takes over. Echoing how she described Alex to Elizabeth at Meryton, she talks about Alex being advanced verbally and how that can be a challenge. "I forget that she's four. I really do. I'll get mad and I'll say, 'Why are you acting like you're four?' Then I stop myself and think, 'Oh yeah. She *is* four.'"

Brianna laughs, seems to relate to that story, writes enthusiastically on the sheet. Brianna asks about Alex's relationship with her brother.

"It's basically very good," Katie says.

"Of course," Miles says, "this morning she built a tower and he knocked it down. She wasn't too happy about that."

"I wouldn't like that either," Brianna says.

"They have the usual sibling stuff," Katie says. "Related to that, Alex's preschool teacher complimented her problem-solving skills during our parent-teacher conference last week. There's this little boy at school who's a bit younger than Alex. She had built a volcano and she was worried that he was gonna knock it down."

"Seems to be a lot of that going around," Brianna says and laughs.

"Exactly," Katie says, joining her. "Why is it that little boys like to knock stuff down?"

"Don't look at me," Miles says.

"So Alex devised this game," Katie says. "She was the mommy and he was the baby. He was all for it. He was so happy to be included in the game with her. Whenever it looked like he was gonna knock down her volcano, she would come up with an activity for him. She'd say, 'You have to go over there and have a nap,' or 'It's snack time. You have to have your snack now.' That type of thing. She was pretty clever. He was able to play with her, she appeased him, it all worked out."

"Very good problem solving. Advanced. And she's very flexible," Brianna says, writing, smiling, and, in this case, underlining something.

Brianna then asks about their involvement in Alex's nursery school.

"I'm very involved," Katie says. "I'm cochair of the PTA, I'm a room parent, and I worked on the annual fund-raiser."

"Wow," Brianna says. "Sounds like a lot."

"I'm happy to do it. It's really not that big a deal. I like to be involved in our kids' school."

The conversation motors along. Any semblance of a structured school interview peels away as they talk further about Katie's involvement at Bright Stars, then about the extracurricular activities at Hunsford, their music program, drama, and dance. Katie asks about Spanish and PE, and after explaining these programs, Brianna asks if they have any questions.

Katie asks what people love the most about Hunsford and what they like least. Brianna pauses, thinks. "I'd say that most of all, people love that we're a community. We're very tight. We're a school, of course, but sometimes we forget that because of the community feel. As for what people complain about . . . you know, it's individual things. And some people are just complainers by nature. I think because we are such a community, the complainers stick out. There is always going to be someone who isn't happy. Nothing's perfect."

Katie and Miles nod in unison.

"Anything else?"

"No," Katie says, looking at Miles, who shrugs. "I don't think so. We totally get it. The truth is, I've been here three times."

"Really?"

"Yeah. I'm not a weirdo or anything. I just love it."

And then Brianna beams.

"What's our next step?" Miles asks, grinning back.

"What happens next is Alex comes for a visit. She hangs out, does a couple of activities, the kindergarten teachers observe her, and that's it, and, well, let's just be positive about this."

"Okay," Katie says.

"Oh, gee, I completely lost track of the time," Brianna says. "We'd better stop."

They stand up, shake hands, and Katie offers what might be, she'll admit, an overly exuberant, overloud thank-you. On the way out of Brianna's office, Katie checks her watch.

They have been with her for an hour and fifteen minutes.

• • •

Driving home with Miles, Katie lets out a sigh and then a whoop.

"That was *great*. Did you hear what she said at the end? *Let's assume it's a yes.*"

"She didn't exactly say that. She said let's be positive."

"Okay. But look, we're very strong candidates. We come from a nursery school that essentially feeds into Hunsford. We're a good family and our kid is a star."

Miles says nothing.

"I know," Katie says. "Lots of families from our school don't get in. I'm just hoping that we're a family that looks right and feels right to them and that Alex wows them when they meet her."

Miles drives. Still says nothing. The silence is crushing her.

"She was so nice," Katie says. "Didn't you think so, Miles? Didn't you think it went well?"

"I did," Miles says. "I think it went really well."

"But?"

"But," Miles says, "you don't know."

"Yeah. It's true. You don't. Jesus, this *sucks*."

"Are you going to write her a thank-you note?"

Katie cracks a smile. "I already did."

Plan B

The Evergreen School sits in the center of the city, swaddled in a small patch of green flanked by a grid of car dealerships, auto body shops, a vacuum cleaner repair shop, a Cuban restaurant, and an animal hospital. The school unfolds in a jumble of cottages, over which spans a concrete walkway leading to a former apartment building, now converted to classrooms. Evergreen feels like 1968 all over again, a place where the music of the Eagles might have been born, where hippies once ruled, where calm and consciousness triumph over test scores and the pressure associated with mountains of elementary school homework. The words murmured most often in these halls are *process* and *holistic*. The motto repeated constantly is "Give a child a fish, he'll eat for a day; teach him how to fish, he'll eat for a lifetime."

Unlike most other schools, Evergreen schedules the child visit before Connie R., director of admissions, or Edgar Mantle, head of the school, meets with the parents.

"I actually think that's smart," Katie says. "They'll meet Alex today and then a week later they'll meet us. That way they can talk to us about her visit."

In the car on the way over, Katie plays down Alex's play date at Evergreen, as she calls it. "We're just gonna check it out. And afterwards we'll talk, you and me, and you'll tell me how it went, what you liked, you know?"

Alex says, "Okay," and looks out the window, past the grid of car dealerships that signals to Katie that they have arrived and that she should find a place to park. She squeezes the SUV into a space in front of an auto body shop, between two wrecked or abandoned cars.

Not jumping up and down over Evergreen's location, she thinks.

On the Evergreen campus, ten prospective kindergartners and their moms meet in the school's library, a large room that reminds Katie of a bed-and-breakfast where she and Miles once stayed in the Berkshires. Connie R. stands off to the side, listening to a prospective mom gush about the school. The mom wears a blue work shirt, jeans, and a buzz cut worthy of k.d. lang. Connie R. nods appreciatively and touches the mom on the shoulder in solidarity. For some reason, the gesture endears Connie to Katie. There is something so unpretentious about her and this school that makes her feel comfortable. Still, she has to admit that Evergreen is not her first choice. It feels less than the others somehow. There are fewer bells and whistles, not as much emphasis on academics, and the parents, both current and prospective, appear more laid-back. To Katie, this all adds up to being undeserving of the price tag the school commands, which is the same as every other private school in the city.

Connie R. moves a few steps into the library and addresses the children in a soft, soothing voice. "Welcome, everyone. I'm so glad you could come. You're going to have a very fun time today. Here's what we're going to do. We're all going to go to a classroom where there are some kids waiting for you. We're going to go in together, you're going to say good-bye to Mommy, and we're going to have circle time. Okay? Let's go."

As the parents file out of the library, Alex slips her hand into Katie's.

"This is going to be cool," Katie says. "You're going to do some fun things like you do at school, there'll be some playtime, then you'll have a snack—"

"I don't want to do circle time," Alex says.

Shit. Why does she hate circle time?

"It'll be fine," Katie says, a plea, but she realizes that Alex has slowed her pace and they are now the last two people to approach the classroom. As Katie reaches the door, Alex pulls on her hand. She pokes her head inside the classroom, and, sure enough, there are a bunch of kids sitting on the rug in a circle. Alex's eyes widen in what Katie knows is panic. Katie stands frozen in the doorway.

What am I going to do? Okay. I have two choices. I can force her into the circle. She will not participate, she will cry, she will kick and scream. Or I can take her outside and talk to her. Either way, Connie will know she's having a freak attack and we're fucked.

And then an angel appears.

A teacher, young, stocky, hair in a bun, a smile that could sell used cars, is leaning over, her face close to Alex in a loving, sympathetic way.

"Hi. My name is Chloe. What's yours?"

"Alex."

"Cool name. Hey, Alex, come on, I'm going to help you sit down next to a nice friend. Your special friend for today. She is way cool, too."

Chloe gently entwines her hand around Alex's little fingers and they are gone, headed into the classroom, where Chloe deposits her onto the rug next to a little girl who grins toothlessly at Alex. Alex looks back at Katie and this time her look of panic has been supplanted by a grin of confidence: *I can do this, Mom. I got this. I'm a big girl.*

Katie blows her a kiss and mouths, "Your snacks are in your pocket."

Alex half-nods. Now that she's in the circle, you have to act like you belong. Gotta be cool. Her new friend grabs her hand, then lets it go as all the kids start to clap to a nursery rhyme led by Chloe, who has taken a chair at the top of the circle.

Katie waits for ten seconds more, then moves back into the library. It's empty for the moment, eerily so. Where have all those other parents gone? No Starbucks within walking distance that she saw.

But Katie is prepared. She reaches into her bag and pulls out her knitting. She is working on a sweater. At least that's her intention. If that doesn't pan out, she'll knit the two sleeves together, or what were supposed to be sleeves, and turn the thing into a blanket. Plan B. Have to have a Plan B. The main thing for today, though, is to keep her hands busy and her mind distracted.

After a while, a couple of the other moms walk in holding Starbucks containers—they must've driven—and sit down across from Katie. It feels as if they are all in a doctor's waiting room or waiting for a repair to be done on their car. One of the moms asks Katie where else she's looking and Katie mentions Meryton, adding a roll of her eyes, and Hunsford, trying to suppress her look of love. The other mom joins the conversation and within minutes they are sharing their fears and frustrations, their concerns and their nervousness. It's instant bonding.

"I don't know what it is," Katie says later. "I just feel very comfortable with the parents at Evergreen. Even the prospective parents seem like my kind of people. I really could be friends with them."

As Katie and the two moms talk, the rest of the prospective parents straggle in. A few minutes later, the imposing school head, Edgar Mantle, flapping a yellow legal pad against his beefy thigh, strides in. He waves the pad at the room.

"Hello. I just wanted to welcome you to Evergreen, and to answer any questions you might have."

Fifteen minutes of the usual. Questions that Katie could by now not only predict but answer.

Q. How many applicants for how many spots?
A. A couple hundred for forty spaces not including siblings. So maybe twenty openings.
Q. What is your homework policy after kindergarten?
A. Three hours a night. I'm kidding. We're more interested in process than in busy work. We do encourage reading at home. I don't know. Maybe thirty minutes a night. Builds up to maybe forty-five minutes by sixth grade.
Q. What are you looking for in a prospective applicant?
A. We're looking to build a community. We want people who see eye to eye with our philosophy, who get who we are. And we're looking for balance. Diversity in every way.

Mantle answers these questions and a few more with patience and humor, putting a lid on his usual theatricality. Then, promising there will be more time for further questions at their interviews, he excuses himself. Katie is impressed. She finds him pleasant and intelligent, says so to her two new friends. Moments later, Chloe comes in. Katie leaps to her feet. "Oh my God. Thank you. You saved my life. You saved my kid's life."

"She was just nervous. It's hard for a lot of kids. They have to adjust to this totally new setting."

"Yeah, but you were incredible. What can I do for you?"

Chloe laughs. "Tell Edgar to give me a raise." She turns to the room. "I actually came in to tell you that the kids are now outside playing. They were all great."

Katie's new friends wait as Katie gathers up her knitting. They walk slowly down the narrow paved path toward the playground, wishing each other good luck and peeling off as soon as they get a glimpse of their kids at play. Katie spots Alex sitting at a snack table with her partner. They are drinking juice boxes and sharing a bag of Goldfish crackers. Katie looks around, counts ten visiting kids with ten kids from Evergreen.

This is a nice way to do it, she thinks.

She starts toward Alex. Alex giggles, says something, and her partner laughs. Katie bends down, smiles at her daughter.

"Hey, kiddo, how you doing?"

A smile, then a sideways glance at her partner. "Good."

"We can go now if you want," Katie says. "Or if you want to stay a little longer, you can. It's up to you."

Alex looks at her new friend, smiles again. "I want to stay for ten more minutes."

"You got it."

"I was surprised," Katie admits later. "I expected that she was going to tell me that she was ready to go back to her school because she loves it so much. I was thrilled that she wanted to stay longer. They give you the option to stay another hour. She went to the max. Had a great time."

In the car on the way home, Katie asks Alex if she likes Evergreen School. "Um-hm," Alex says.

"What did you like best about it?"

Alex presses her nose against the window, thinks. "The playground," she says. "And the kids."

"Cool. It's a good school, huh?"

"Um-hm."

Well, okay. At least I have a reference point, Katie thinks as she pulls into her driveway. *But man . . . a few months ago I would not have put Evergreen on the map for us. It's perfectly fine. But it's not Hunsford. If I don't get in there, I don't know what I'll do.*

Katie's Dream

The next week, Katie and Miles have interviews at Warwick and Bingley, two schools they rank behind Meryton and, of course, Hunsford, which has emerged in Katie's mind as more than her first choice; it has become her quest, her Holy Grail, as Miles puts it, "her heart's desire." After the interviews, Katie and Miles are prepared to eliminate both Warwick and Bingley, but for different reasons.

Warwick reminds Miles of the public school he attended. The building is nondescript, the teachers seem exhausted, the kids listless. The interview is a chore for them as well as for the admissions director, who barely looks up from their application. Katie manages to feign a degree of enthusiasm for the school, but Miles says maybe two sentences in the entire forty-five minutes they spend imprisoned on the admissions director's couch.

"I just think we need choices," Katie says, breaking the five-minute silence in the car on the way home.

"I will send Alex to our public school before I'll spend a dime sending her to Warwick," Miles says.

"I didn't hate it that much."

"Hate is too strong a word. Let's go with detest or loathe."

In contrast, Bingley is a marvel of concrete and glass, featuring facilities that rival many colleges and a school head who regularly publishes in respected educational journals. Although Bingley is relatively new, it has become the hottest school in the city, Trina, who has her pulse on everything, tells Katie. But it takes Katie thirty-three minutes to get there door-to-door, and coming back in midmorning traffic takes her almost an hour.

"I can't do that every day, twice a day," she moans to Trina. "I have two kids. I'll be living in my car."

"Great school," Trina says.

"Hunsford is a great school and it's five minutes from my house."

"Here's the thing," Trina says. She pauses.

"What? I hate when you pause. It's never a good thing."

"Okay." Another pause.

"What?"

"I know of four kids from our class who are already *in* Hunsford. Three girl sibs and one boy sib. That's four right away. Last year they took eight kids from our school. I know of at least ten who are applying this year, six girls, including Alex. They've already taken three girls. They're not gonna take nine girls from Bright Stars."

Now Katie pauses. "So what you're saying is it's not looking good."

"I'm saying you have to really push Gracie. She's the director of our preschool. She has to know how much you want it."

"I've gotten this whole damn Hunsford thing stuck in my head. I'm thinking I'm getting in there and now you're telling me I'm not."

"I'm telling you it's going to be tough."

"I have to meet with Gracie and figure out Plan B. I need to get my head into that. What if Hunsford doesn't happen? What is my Plan B?"

．　　．　　．

In the dream, Katie is waiting for the mail. She is sitting on the living room couch beneath the window. Suddenly the light flickers and dims and it is night. She hears footsteps and then she is jarred by a loud thud of letters and packages landing outside her front door.

She is standing now over the mail. She bends down and rummages through a mound of envelopes, magazines, and bills. She finally comes to the five envelopes she has been waiting for, one from each school. Two of the envelopes are thick, two are thin, and one, the one she holds in her hand, is lumpy. She opens that one first.

Inside is a pile of vomit.

She wakes up in a sea of sweat, her stomach taut with nausea.

CHAPTER SIX

Failing at Four

The kids visit and we observe them. We're not
evaluating them, grading them, or testing them.
Four-year-olds should not be tested. Period.

—*a head of a private school*

ERB

With few exceptions, every child who applies for private
school kindergarten in the United States is in some way tested.
Even a school like Meryton, the rarity that never meets its applicants, relies on the oral and written evaluations of the child's
preschool. According to Elizabeth Marx, director of admissions, the Meryton philosophy is summed up with the statement
"We've never met a four-year-old we haven't liked." But they
have met *forty*-year-olds they haven't liked. As Elizabeth Marx
says, "The nursery school teachers know your child and the
nursery school directors know you."

Almost every private school in New York City requires
kindergarten candidates to take a single standardized test, commonly called the ERB. ERB stands for the Educational Records
Bureau, which is a nonprofit organization that administers and
interprets many different types of tests given to students from

preschool through high school. The test that applicants for kindergarten take is always the latest version of what's known as the WPPSI (Wechsler Preschool and Primary Scale of Intelligence). The test is given in approximately fifty preschools throughout New York City and at the offices of the ERB in midtown Manhattan. The ERB test is administered by a staff of approximately forty trained examiners, most with degrees in psychology, some with PhDs. The tests are given privately, one-on-one, examiner to child. Usually the child and examiner sit at a table. The examiner asks a list of questions and records the child's answers on an answer sheet with a range from 1 to 99, a score calculated as a result of how the child has responded to the same questions in comparison to other children his or her age throughout the country. In addition to the numerical scores, the test includes a narrative, a running commentary in which the examiner describes the child's behavior during the test. Parents and admissions directors find the narrative a telling part of the report, especially when a numerical score is less than desirable and needs explaining. The test itself is divided into two parts, verbal and performance. Within each of these two parts are four or five subparts that assess specific levels of development in areas such as arithmetic, vocabulary, and picture completion.

Although Pemberley School is not located in New York City, Dana Optt sees the value of a developmentally appropriate test. "It comes down to evaluating a lot of different things. What is a child's fine motor like with a pencil? Can she listen to a story? Can she remember something that she heard in a story? Can she discriminate visually between two or three things? The examiner will ask, 'Pick this pencil up. Put it on the desk. Put it on the floor.' Part of it is listening and following directions. You can readily find out who has difficulty processing language, which tells you who's going to struggle in school because of a learning disability.

"Here's another example from the test, or at least a type of question," she says. "I'll say, 'I'm gonna say a word and I want you to listen.' I say baseball. 'Now you say the word. Now say it again, but don't say ball.' It's a very developmental thing. Can the kid take it in, can he listen to the direction, and can he separate the two words? That is what he's gonna have to do in kindergarten. That's a pre-reading skill. Here's another example from the test. You say to the kid, 'You need gasoline for your car to run. You need a pilot to fly a plane. What do you need to work a television?' You hear everything from 'You need to plug it in' to 'You need a little black box' to 'I think you need TiVo.'

"I believe there's merit to giving kids the ERB test because it can tell you what they're thinking. I also believe that the stress associated with taking the test comes from the parents. In most cases, kids take the test in their own preschool, in their own environment. It's comfortable. It's fun. The kids like it. They really do. All their friends are taking it. Kids do talk. Even in preschool. The other thing is, after the test, the results are mailed, you read the narrative, and you can meet with the psychologists who will tell you, 'These are the things your child is very strong in and these are the things your child needs help with.' They cover a wide range: social interaction, social cues, and so on. Finally, it's humane. The child takes one test, one time. You don't have to drag your child to ten different schools to go through ten different evaluations. To me, that's not fair."

The head of a prestigious private school in New York sees the ERBs as less important than parents think.

"The ERB is a small factor in our decision-making. If the scores correspond to other factors, then it carries more weight. If the scores are out of whack compared to what we see and what the preschool says, we know that the child just had a bad day. It's not that important to us. I'm not saying that it isn't important at other schools. It could be. To me, it's one more stress thing. You have to put it in perspective, realize it's really just a snapshot. The bottom line is it's hard to assess a four-year-old. There are certain developmental markers that you look for, then you have to really look at the family. You want to make sure that the parents buy into what the school gives them and that, above all, they are reasonable people. You're taking a chance. Unless there are clear indicators, it is a large leap of faith."

MK, director of admissions at Longbourne, says, "The ERB evolved in an interesting way. From what I understand, every school in New York used to do their own thing. The kids were being evaluated left and right. Everybody at the time felt that was completely inappropriate. So there was a movement toward giving one test to every kid, and the ERB evolved. Now, that's the way it's supposed to be, but it doesn't really happen that way. You're not supposed to be testing kids when they come on their visits, but every school gives some kind of evaluation of their own to see how kids work. It's not like they're doing test-type things. Hopefully. But I know that some people do more stuff than others. The ERB is supposed to be the one test kids are given, period. And, yes, it is an IQ test. However, it's not accurate to judge IQ until age seven. So if the ERB is an IQ test, it is in only a moment of time for a young child. You must take that into consideration when you're looking at the results. As a director of admissions, I consider the ERB to be just one piece of the pie. And you really have to know how to read the thing. It's kind of like those allergy blood tests. When it's positive, it's positive. But when it's negative, it doesn't necessarily mean that you don't have the allergy. It is a little bit like that. Chances are if a strength shows up on the test, it is indeed a strength. But a weakness may not be a weakness. These things shift over time. Every school in the city puts a different weight on the ERB test. I will say this, however: if you have a test with all very low scores, you may have something to worry about. Chances are the child has some kind of issue. I think the test correlates that much. It's very unusual for a child to bomb the test and for there not to be a problem. Still, you really do have to consider every factor. For example, you might be dealing with separation issues when a child takes the test. I do think a child who's missing her mommy is going to have a really hard time. As a result, I think your scores are less accurate."

MK continues, "The ERB results have a lot of parts. The first page is basically the scores, the numbers. The second page is the write-up. Parents will often turn around and say, 'Oh, my child is wonderful. The tester said he's so great. Everything's perfect.' And I want to say, 'Have you ever heard of liability?' The testers are afraid of being sued by some irate, insane lawyer parent. So you are never going to see much accuracy on that second page. It's starting to get a little better. I happen to think that the testers shouldn't be that honest. You don't want a parent walking around thinking that his or her child is not wonderful. Unfortunately, that happens all the time. The ERB results come in and if the scores don't hit a certain number, parents will look at their kids differently. I've heard of cases in which a parent's relationship with their kid changes as a result of the ERB test. Until they took the test, they thought their kid was brilliant. Now the kid gets in the eightieth percentile and the parents think the kid is a lesser person or something. It's terrible. That's why the ERB examiners are so careful about what they write on that second page. They don't want to get sued. I'm serious! The whole thing sickens me. Can you imagine your relationship with your kid changing because of what he gets on a *test*? You know what I really think? We shouldn't have ERBs. We shouldn't have SATs. We shouldn't have any of that. I would do away with all those standardized tests. Immediately."

We Were Pleased

On a murderously cold day in January, Shea Cohen sits in her Upper East Side living room sipping tea. Bundled up in a heavy sweater, she wraps both hands around her cup. Liam's ERB results and report lie facedown on the coffee table in front of her.

"If the ERB scores aren't good, people freak out." Shea blows on her tea, sips. "What you hope in that case is that the schools you're applying to have really good rapport with your nursery school director. You do hear that certain schools have cutoff numbers. Some schools, the really academic ones, supposedly only take kids in the nineties. Then you hear that this kid scored in the eighties and got in. It's all part of the urban myth. Mysterious. Frustrating. Annoying."

Shea puts her tea down on the coffee table, using the current *New Yorker* as a coaster.

"I have a friend who has a son Liam's age. He and Liam are pals. He has an older brother at Longbourne so he's a sib. He's already in. Done deal. My friend and I made a bet. She said, 'I'll bet you a dollar that Liam scores in the ninety-ninth percentile.'"

Shea shrugs, picks up her cup. "What's funny is the preschool doesn't tell you when the test is. You have no idea. One day your kid comes home with a note saying, 'Your child had his ERB test today.' But the kids talk. They are aware of everything. Like one day Liam came home and said, 'My friend went to Hurst Academy today. When am I going to visit Hurst Academy?' I said, 'You're not going to Hurst Academy.'"

Shea leans forward on the couch and, in an impression of Liam, puts both hands on her hips and raises her voice slightly.

"Well, why not?"

"Because, Liam, there's like a hundred schools out there. We're not going to look at every single one. Everybody looks at different schools and we picked the ones we thought would be right for you."

Shea circles her hands around her cup again and comes out of her Liam impression. "Luckily he didn't ask, 'Why not?' I would've had to make up some bullshit answer like, 'It's too far from our apartment.' It's the same thing with the ERBs."

Cup down. Back to Liam again.

"When am I going in to see the lady? When am I going to go?"

"'Soon, Liam, I promise. You'll go soon. Everybody's going to get a chance.' And when he did go, he didn't even tell me. At least I got the note. I said, 'You saw the lady today.'"

"Yep."

"How was it?"

"It was fun."

"So you had a good time?"

"Yeah. I had a good time. A lot of those questions were very easy. There were a couple that were a little harder."

"I left it at that. They go into the library. They sit at a table. The tester sits there with a sheet and they go through it. So let's see."

She flips over the test results and looks them over.

"They do vocabulary. Similarities. The verbal part has four subtests and the performance part also has four subtests. You have coding. I think that's the only test that's timed. You have, for example, a picture of a car, a dog, and a house. Under the car is a red square, under the dog is a purple circle, and so on. Then they have the same pictures below, maybe in a different order. The kids are supposed to figure out the code. So, it's like, okay, the house is a yellow circle, you put that over here. Almost like matching. Then there's block design. The tester will make something out of blocks, or maybe it's already there on a piece of paper. Say it's a star, whatever. The kid then has to make the same design. It's like those Mighty Mind things. It's testing small motor and I guess the ability to perceive. I don't know."

Shea peers at the ERB results, nods once. "So this is the narrative. *'Liam is enthusiastic and attentive and his big smile, striking blond hair, sparkling blue eyes, and outgoing chatter marked the session.'* They have such a way with phrasing. It's all like that. Very positive. There is an element of this that borders on the ridiculous. *'Liam settled into the new situation readily. Rapport was established immediately. Self-assured, he moved from test to test rapidly. Liam quickly grasped the intent of each task, at times pre-empting the complete instructions. He watched the examiner's demonstrations with the hands-on items attentively and followed through with work directly.'* It gets better."

And Shea reads, "*'Liam enjoyed verbal interchange both in casual conversation and in response to guided questions. Excellent command of word meanings; defined many words on a vocabulary list with precise, succinct statements. Liam rapidly assigned abstract categories to sets of word pairs, recognized the underlying commonalities in the relationships. A very fine problem solver. Listening to successive verbal clues, he used deductive reasoning skills to identify a concept. Readily changed his mind with new in-*

formation. Liam has absorbed much from the world around him, offering several suggestions for practical everyday social dilemmas.'"

Shea looks up, does a comical double take.

"I'm like, *what?* He needs to do that at home. Whenever I have a dilemma and I'd like a suggestion, all I get is screaming and crying. A fine problem solver? Maybe they confused him with another kid."

Shea returns to the narrative, picking up the pace, reading at twice normal speed. *"'Using a conventional right-handed pencil grip, Liam copied several rows of symbols to match a code. Eager to share an anecdote, he interrupted his work using several seconds . . .'"*

Shea laughs. "Okay, now that's him. He was probably in the middle of the test and he stopped to tell a story. He's Mr. Anecdote." And Shea channels Liam again: *"You know this coding thing reminds me of a funny story. When we were in the rain forest one summer, our guide Gerardo—"*

She looks back at the narrative. *"'Liam responded to cajoling and returned to task.'"* Shea rolls her eyes, reads: *"'With a keen eye, he could picture groups based on their common properties, getting some of the later, more subtle ones after missing some of the earlier, easy ones. Excellent spatial organizational abilities. With no wasted motions, he assembled both simple and bipolar block patterns. Kept his eye on the model and picture as he noted block positions. Persevered up to a point. Realistic when success was not in sight. Completed many matrices with a quick grasp of inherent analogies.'* That is pretty much the test. Then there are some general comments. *'Liam had very good attention and strong stamina throughout the hour. He seemed to have fun trying his hand at each task. He moved from activity to activity with ease. It was a delight to work with Liam. His confidence and comfort in the situation contributed to a very smooth and enjoyable session. He is clearly a child with outstanding strengths in both the verbal and performance domain. Abstract thinking ability and visual motor skill are particularly noteworthy.'* So that is it."

Shea sighs and tosses the ERB results onto the coffee table.

"Usually people are very tight-lipped about the test. It's a little like asking how much money you make. It's very personal and bad form to ask outright. What happens is, someone will say, 'Did you get the scores back yet? How did he do? Did he do okay?' And you're like, 'Yeah. He did well. We were pleased.' Then again, I think a lot of people lie."

Shea breaks into her upturned smile. "I was pleased," she says. "In fact, I owe my friend a dollar."

The Test

The woman in black sits in the school's library with six other women in black, accompanied by their sidekicks, men in black, fidgety and superior, annoyed that they've been forced here on a Saturday. Some of the men speak on cell phones, some read the sports section, all avoid eye contact. The women speak to each other in muted, grave voices as if dispensing classified information. They are recovering from a twenty-minute speech and fifteen-minute question-and-answer session with the head of the school, a plump, balding man in a rumpled suit. He spoke glowingly of his school, of course, through a smile that seemed snapped on, like a pair of fake plastic lips you might find in a costume store. He is a polished speaker, so polished that what he said felt too glib, too practiced. Through it all, the hype about the school, the insincere smile, the canned speech, the woman in black detected a whiff of arrogance, a dark underside to what was presented as a pure and fluffy whipped-cream cloud.

I suppose I can't blame him, she thinks. *I mean, look at us. Seven des-*

perate housewives, most of us, I'll bet, graduates of top-tier colleges, some with advanced or law degrees, seated next to our moneyed, powerful husbands, while our kids are scrutinized in the next room by a team of four kindergarten teachers and one schlumpy admissions director, women of lesser intelligence, means, and prominence, but who this morning are not only our equals, they hold the key to our children's futures. Once my kid is in, I'll kick the shit out of them, but today I'll kiss their asses collectively in Bloomingdale's window if that's what it takes. And looking around at the other thirteen rich, powerful, elite women and men in black, she thinks, *So would they.*

But this Saturday morning, her son, call him Brian, holds all the cards. He is the one they're watching. He is the one about whom they'll raise their thumbs up or down. They have given their all in this game, left nothing to chance, made the right calls, said all the right things, winked in all the right places. The woman in black folds her hands in her lap.

The game is now his to lose. We have bred him well. He will not fail us.

It comes down to one simple test.

A test designed to separate the leaders from the flock. To weed out the strong from the weak.

"Our kindergarten is made up of tomorrow's world leaders."

That is what the school head said. And that is truly what he and the woman in black believe.

The children have been allowed five minutes of free play in the school playground, after which they've been promised a snack. While the three boys in their Ralph Lauren Polo shirts and khaki pants and the four girls in their Gap dresses navigate the ins and outs of the school's play structure, a multilevel redwood thing resembling a mini A-frame in Napa, the kindergarten teachers set five chairs around a table. At the head of the table they arrange seven plates of cookies and seven juice boxes.

When they've finished, one of the teachers tinkles a small bell and in a pleasant but insistent voice calls, "Snack time!"

The children abandon their positions on the play structure and arrive at the table, which is set beneath a metal overhang.

"Line up now," the teacher says. "Single file." The three other teachers and director of admissions watch, foreheads furrowed, clipboards at the ready, pens poised.

The children line up, eager for a snack. One boy, the third in line, looks with concern at the number of chairs. His lips moving, his finger pointing, he calculates that there are more children than chairs.

"Here you go."

The teacher hands him his cookies and juice. The little boy hesitates, sees one little girl already seated at the table, and decides then to make a sacrifice, to take one for the team. He will give his place at the table to somebody else. He will find somewhere else to sit. Holding his snack and drink in front of him, he sees a shady spot in front of a tree. The little boy sits down there, alone, and begins to munch on a cookie.

Brian is next in line. He receives his plate of cookies and his juice box and offers a polite "Thank you" to the teacher who passes them out. He, too, observes that the table has only five chairs, two of which are now taken. And then Brian sees the little boy sitting off by himself.

He looks kind of lonely, Brian thinks. *And there's really not enough room around the table, anyway. I'll keep him company.*

Wordlessly, he joins the little boy in his spot by the tree. Silently, the two boys enjoy their snack, watching the table fill up in the distance, happy that they've managed to find their own spot and that they didn't have to get anyone in trouble for not finding a seat at the table. Brian feels quite proud of himself. He could've grabbed his cookies and juice and slammed his butt down onto a chair, as if he were a contestant in a vicious version of musical chairs. But, no, this is school. You're supposed to co-operate. He did a good job. He did the right thing.

On the way home, Brian tells his parents how he sat with the other little boy under the tree, choosing not to sit at the table with the others.

He finishes his story. Instead of praise there is silence.

"Tell me you didn't really do that," his mother says, her voice trembling a little. His father stares ahead, his fingers gripping the steering wheel of the Mercedes.

"There was no room. I didn't want to cause any trouble."

"You didn't want to cause any—" The woman in black glares at her husband. "I don't believe this. Did you hear that?"

"I heard."

The woman in black whirls around to her son, who is strapped into his car seat in the backseat. "Why did you do that? Tell me!"

"I thought—"

"You were supposed to sit at the table! You were supposed to be part of the group! Not sit under a tree! It was a *test*."

Brian sniffs once and starts to cry.

"Aw, fuck," the woman in black says. She whips her head back, faces the road ahead, unclasps her purse, and yanks out a crumpled Kleenex. She blows her nose so violently that it causes both her husband and Brian to jump.

"Fuck," she says again.

Her husband says nothing. In the backseat, Brian whimpers. He doesn't dare cry out loud.

Two months later the woman in black will receive a letter from the school assigning Brian to the gulag known as the waitlist.

Liam's Visit

The night before his visit at Longbourne, Shea Cohen gives Liam two choices of shirts to go with his khaki pants: a blue button-down oxford or a dark green turtleneck.

"Not the turtleneck," Liam says. "The tag itches and bothers me. I don't like the turtleneck."

"That settles that," Shea says.

Sitting in the admissions office the next morning, Shea, Donald, and Liam watch as a boy in an apparently very itchy turtleneck comes out of MK's office and heads over to his parents.

"How was it?" the mom asks. "Did you have fun?"

"Can I take this shirt off now?" the boy pleads, shoving his fingers underneath the cloth that throttles his neck.

Shea winks at Liam and Liam covers his mouth with both hands, stifling a laugh. MK speaks to the boy's parents for a few minutes, then disappears into the office. The boy and his family leave, lugging with them an anvil of anxiety. A moment later MK bounds out of the office and heads toward the Cohen family.

"Okay, which one of you is Liam?"

Liam shoots his hand into the air. "I am."

"You are? Are you sure?"

Liam laughs. "I'm sure."

"Amazing. That was the first question I had and you knew the answer! You're doing great! So here's the plan. You and I are going to go into my office, right there where your mom and dad can see you, and we're gonna have a talk. I'm going to ask you some even trickier questions like, 'What's your name?' Oh. You already answered that one. Okay. 'How old are you?'"

Another big laugh and a look toward Shea that reads, *Is this person for real?* then to MK, "That's not a tricky question. That's an easy question."

"Really? I'm gonna have to think of something harder. Oh, I almost forgot. At the end of our talk, you're going to get a prize. Something great if you answer all my questions and, okay, something great even if you don't."

MK offers a hand. Liam grabs it happily and they go off, chatting away.

"No problem with transition there," Donald says.

"I can see his high school yearbook now," Shea says. "Most likely to join a cult."

Liam and MK are back in less than twenty minutes. Liam is holding a ball. He giggles at something MK says.

"Look, Mom, look at this." Liam bounces the ball. The inside lights up.

"Wow. Very cool."

"Well, Liam, I certainly had a good time," MK says. "Did you?"

"Yep."

"It was delightful meeting you."

MK extends a hand. Liam takes it. MK shakes his hand vigorously, pumping it up and down. Without letting go, MK says, "I hope you had fun meeting me."

"Yep."

Still MK shakes his hand. "Oh, good, because I want the kids I visit with to have a good time. I was worried there."

MK *still* shakes his hand and now Liam is laughing, his small body jouncing as if it were made of Jell-O.

"Liam, what's the matter?"

"You won't stop shaking my hand!"

"Are you kidding? You won't let go of mine!"

Liam tries to pull away but MK continues to shake his hand, and now Liam is hysterical with laughter, practically doubled over, and then MK and Donald and Shea start laughing, too, until MK, pretending to use superhuman force, finally pulls away.

"What a handshake!"

Liam is gasping for breath, he's laughing so hard. And as he gains control, MK, standing over him, mouths silently to Donald and Shea, "I love him."

CHAPTER SEVEN

All About Me, Sweetheart

A good recommendation from a nursery school that I respect is a strong place to start.

—*a head of a private school*

I have one word to say about feeder nursery schools: *bullshit*.

—*an educational consultant*

Feeding the Beast

Are there really such things as feeder nursery schools?

Every school head and admissions director I spoke to acknowledged that the relationship with each applicant's preschool is one of the key elements in the kindergarten admissions process.

Every preschool director I spoke to denied this.

Preschool directors repeated, "I *wish* I had the power to get my kids in; I don't," so often that it rang in my ears like an anthem. *Plausible deniability*, I thought every time I heard it. Educational consultants echoed the refrain like backup singers.

"Preschool directors deny that there are feeder nursery schools, but I know what I hear from parents," one educational

135

consultant said. "The ones who have their kids in those schools sure believe it."

Another educational consultant insisted, "There is no such animal as a feeder nursery school. A family will get in or not get in because of the *family*. It doesn't matter where the kid goes to nursery school."

But school heads and directors of admissions in all innocence and honesty pulverized these claims; one clearly articulated why the relationship with the preschool is so important: "Yes, there are some nursery schools that are feeders. I hate the notion of it, but it's just a fact. And over the years, patterns are repeated. We happen to live in a city where there are a lot of very good nursery schools. I want to emphasize that going to a nursery school that I don't know well does not in any way rule somebody out. But knowing certain nursery schools helps. I know how a child has been brought along. I have a sense of what the family feels toward education, and the feeling that we're all in the same boat, committed to the same things. You know if they *get* it. A good recommendation from a nursery school that I respect is a strong place to start."

Why then would preschool directors and educational consultants vehemently deny the notion of feeder nursery schools? One reason might lie in the preschool directors' desire to create the illusion that they actually have little power when it comes to affecting admissions decisions. By diminishing their own power in the eyes of the parents, preschool directors take the pressure off getting children into certain top-tier kindergartens as they strengthen the likelihood that other children will get into lower-tier schools. Of course, some preschool directors might enjoy basking in the glory of something akin to celebrity status, but this comes with a risk. If a preschool director alleges to have the ability to get children into certain schools but ultimately fails, the bubble bursts, credibility is shot, enrollment may suffer.

"There is a nursery school in the city whose director claims that she will get them in," an educational consultant said. "Last year a family who applied to eight elementary schools got into only their *last* choice. This director made the mistake of calling those parents a few days before and saying, 'You're in all of them. Don't worry.' Rumor has it that the mother threatened to *sue* the director of this nursery school for misleading them, calling it breach of promise. Not good."

Additionally, educational consultants, at least one of whom reportedly charges $6,000 per family for her services, maintain that preschool directors have little or no power. While I can't deny that educational consultants serve a purpose for some people, this seems like a blatantly transparent attempt to preserve their own business. If the most important relationship in the process is that of the ongoing school's director of admissions and the preschool director, it would appear that an independent educational consultant would become a third wheel, left out of the loop.

New York mom Shea Cohen, a savvy Manhattan private school prospective parent, explained the relationship from the parents' perspective. "The way it works is—or so you hear—the nursery school director will talk with the ongoing school. That conversation matters a lot. Your preschool director has to champion your cause. These schools talk to each other. When all the pieces are in, when we've finished all our interviews, when we've gotten the ERBs back, we'll sit down with our director and she will say, 'All right. Name the four places where you'll be happy. And name one where you'll be *ecstatic*.' Let's be honest. For the money we'll be paying, I want to be ecstatic."

While the exact power a preschool director has in placing children in certain kindergartens remains nebulous (that is, known to some but kept secret from the public), it is disingenuous for any preschool director not to admit, even grudgingly, that her voice in the process matters, and sometimes mightily. Naturally all preschools or preschool directors are not created equal and therefore not all voices command the same degree of influence. But a preschool director's opinion and the school's teachers' evaluations are crucial pieces of the puzzle.

"You have to keep in mind that every kid is an unwritten book," an admissions director said. "These are four-year-olds who are still very much in the process of forming and developing. I rely on what the preschool says and I depend on the preschool to be honest. I have respect for a preschool director who says to me, 'I think you have a greater risk with this child than with that one.' Of course, they have to be diplomatic. They have to be truthful with us and helpful to the parents. Tough position to be in. Very tough."

Depending on the school and the city, the role of the preschool director in the kindergarten admissions process can range from being a respected adviser to a silent partner. In New York, where the levels of intensity, panic, and desperation in the process outpace all other cities, the relationship between the ongoing school and preschool is considered crucial, with some calling it incestuous. Everywhere else, preschool directors are at a minimum kept constantly informed. A director of admissions at a school located in a city other than New York said, "I have continual conversations with nursery school directors. They get very anxious as it gets closer to the letters going out. They want to know has anything changed from the initial status we've given them. I'm obligated to them and I do my best to keep them in the loop."

At Pemberley School, Dana Optt disputed the notion of feeder nursery schools and offered this scenario. "I talk to preschool directors before my acceptance list goes out. Actually, I'll talk to them by January and I'll be very specific with them. I'll say, 'Look, I'm gonna be taking very few boys. I have so many sibling applicant boys this year. You really should push them to other schools to make sure they have a place. Be very careful with boys.' Or, 'This is a year where I have tons of diversity applications.' I'm honest.

"A couple of years ago I told them, 'I don't think I'm going to take any boys at all.' The response was insane. People were screeching all over town. But at least I let them know in advance who I was taking and what the situation was. It's not fair for them to be sitting there the Monday morning after the letters go out saying, 'I don't know why so-and-so didn't get in.' It's not fair to the parents, and it's not fair to the preschool directors.

"The parents need the preschool directors to hold their hands through this. They have to be able to say, 'Listen, I talked to Dana. She was really disappointed that she couldn't let your family in. It was just a narrow spot. It was a big year for faculty, for diversity.' That's better than having Gracie at Bright Stars saying, 'I have no idea what happened at Pemberley.'

"I know that some schools like to keep this veil of mystery going. I don't believe in that. I think it's important to be as up front as possible with parents and preschools. This whole process is built on relationships. To start with, I need to be able to trust the preschool directors. One time I had a conversation with a preschool director who had sent me her list. I knew from a parent here that someone on the list was a nightmare. I called the director on it. I said, 'Why would you send me people who are difficult? You wouldn't do that, would you?' She said, 'Let me redo the list.'"

Recently, two new trends have emerged, both inevitable, one in particular disturbing. In New York, proving once again that Manhattan is the hub of the private school admissions process, a few preschools have hired "*exmissions* directors," whose sole responsibility is to help place children at ongoing schools.

"If I wanted to, I could devote all of my time to the kindergarten application process," a preschool director told me. "It has become that consuming, both in time and in energy. Forget curriculum, dealing with problems of parents, students, teachers . . . forget it. I need another *me*."

I encountered the second predictable and disturbing trend when I spoke to a friend who had just had a baby. Although she was four years away from applying to private school kindergarten, she was concerned that she was already shut out. I asked if she'd ever heard of feeder nursery schools.

"Are you kidding? They're impossible to get into," she said. "You have to first get into a feeder Mommy & Me. And in order to get into one of those, you have to call the moment your kid is born, like from the hospital."

"You're serious."

"Absolutely. I waited until Tyler was three weeks old. Too late. The Mommy & Me I wanted was already full. There's a waiting list. Maybe somebody will drop out. Otherwise, I don't know what we're going to do."

Is this where we're headed? *In order to get into Harvard, your child has to get into the right Mommy & Me?*

Or is that where we are?

Fuckly

For each Saturday visit at Pemberley, Dana Optt recruits fifteen faculty members to evaluate the thirty children who attend. The tests begin as soon as the children arrive; Dana and her team surreptitiously scribble on their evaluation forms even while the children are waiting to be called into the classrooms. They take careful note of who is sitting in a parent's lap, who needs time to get warmed up, who is eager to jump right into an activity, and who is shy and requires more time to adjust to new surroundings. Ultimately what they are looking for are kids who can be part of a group and are willing to collaborate.

One of the exercises Dana relies on involves a simple picture. The teachers give each child the same picture to look at, a drawing of a boy in front of an ice-cream store. There's a dog in front. Dana asks, "What do you think is going on here?"

Some kids say, "Dog, store, boy."

Which is the wrong answer. Dana is looking for three complete thoughts. The child who is on target will say, "There is a doggie in front of the store," or "The boy is going into the store," or "The boy is buying ice cream." In contrast to what many parents believe, the number of sounds and letters a child knows has nothing to do with how well that child will read. Reading readiness has much more to do with the processing of language.

"I had a kid who lived in one of the poorest, roughest parts of town," Dana says. "He looked at that picture and said, 'I think the boy is going to rob the store.' That kid had an amazing processing of language."

This test to Dana is a great equalizer. "I've had kids from the fanciest parts of town going, 'Dog, boy, store.' I'll call their preschool afterwards and ask, 'Did their language come in late?

They don't seem to be connecting things together.' It's all about the language. That is the key for us. That tells me if someone is going to struggle with reading."

Dana divides the faculty into two groups: observers and facilitators. As the children work through their tests, the observers fill out forms, making judgments, assessing behavior, always keeping in mind that four-year-olds are unpredictable and that this is an artificial environment. Dana is looking for extremes, children who can't engage, kids who act out, kids who manifest obvious learning differences.

"I know that as kids go through school, there will be something. There always is. I have never seen a kid who didn't have an issue. But some kids have problems. There's a difference. The Saturday visit often identifies those kids."

The evaluation takes about an hour. The kids move from table to table in different classrooms, working on a variety of skills.

"I look at fine motor," Dana says. "We ask the kids to do some drawing. It's all developmental stuff. We're not asking kids, 'Can you recognize these letters? Can you read? Do you know these sounds?' It's much more about thinking. We'll ask some analogies. I have worked with some of the best educational therapists in the city. We've created the test with the intent of trying to see how a child will do in elementary school; it's not about how much a child knows now."

The other benefit of these Saturday evaluations is that Dana has the opportunity to interact with the children, away from their parents. Over the years Dana has learned that children are open, blunt, and uncensored.

A four-year-old boy once said to her, "This is a very nice school. What do you have for lunch?"

"We have pretty good food here," Dana said. "Lots of different things."

"Well, my parents really want me to go to Meryton. Do you know if they have good lunches there?"

"I hear they're delicious," Dana said. "And I love the people there. They're very nice."

"Really? Great. Because that's where I'm going."

"I wish I could've been in their car on the way home," Dana said later with a sly smile.

Another time a sad-faced five-year-old said to Dana, "My father will not let me have any guns to play with. But if you say I did a good job today, he's taking me to Toys 'R' Us and buying me a big gun. And my mom said I can have anything else I want."

"What about me? I think I did a pretty good job," Dana said. "Can I come with you?"

•   •   •

In bed, as the local news leads into Leno's monologue, Lauren and Craig Pernice talk about analogies.

"Dana told us in our interview that they show the kids a picture," Lauren says. "I presume they're looking for the difference between the kids who say, 'Dog, cat, yard' and the kids who say, 'Hey, that dog is chasing the cat through the yard.' I think that's what they're looking for, a narrative of some kind."

"She also mentioned verbal analogies," Craig reminds her.

"You mean SAT-type analogies?"

"I would assume so."

"That's a pretty advanced skill for a four-year-old," Lauren says.

Craig nods, then looks up at the ceiling for a moment.

"What's on your mind?"

Craig shrugs, reaches over, and clicks off the light by the side of the bed.

The next morning Craig comes in to breakfast holding an envelope. He grins at Killian, who sits at the table, slurping cereal.

"Hey, Killian, check this out," Craig says and shows him the envelope. On it he'd written, "Foot: shoe, head: blank."

"Oh my God," Lauren says. She blows a small torrent of air upward, causing her bangs to flutter on her forehead.

"So, Killian, if shoe goes after foot, what goes after head?"

Killian stares at the envelope.

"Think about it," says Craig. "Foot, shoe, head—"

"Hat?"

"You got it!"

"The analogies could be *pictures* for all we know," Lauren says, her southern accent leaking out. "It may be the kind of thing you see on kids' menus. It might not be these SAT things at all."

"It doesn't really matter. It's about getting comfortable with the format. That's all it is."

"Encouraging and developing test-taking skills in preschool, is that what we're doing here?"

Craig pours a cup of coffee. "If he's being tested, what's wrong with a little coaching from his parents?"

"Nothing. Or we could just leave him alone and say, 'It will be what it will be.'"

Craig looks at her through a slim smile, which, translated, says, *I'm not about to do that.*

•   •   •

The morning of his Pemberley visit, Lauren pours Killian's cereal into a bowl.

"No," Craig says.

Lauren stops midpour. "No?"

"You need to give him a protein breakfast. Studies have shown that people think better on a protein breakfast."

"You're kidding, right?"

"I'm serious. He's got to have protein."

Lauren stares at Craig. Craig meets her eyes. He's serious. Lauren shrugs. Cereal back into the cabinet, she quickly scrambles two eggs and pops two pieces of bread into the toaster. Killian picks at the eggs, devours the toast. As Lauren clears the table, Craig leaves the kitchen. He returns moments later with a comb and hair gel.

"We have to comb his hair," he says. "His hair is unruly. He looks so much better with his hair combed."

Lauren lays the dishes in the sink, whirls around, and barricades herself between her son and her husband.

"Lauren, what are you doing? Get out of my way."

"No hair gel," she says.

Craig studies his wife. Her eyes have become wide brown circles. "Lauren, I want to comb his hair," he pleads.

"No hair gel, Craig. Do not put hair gel in my son's hair."

"Why not?"

"BECAUSE IT LOOKS STUPID!"

Craig pauses. He's not sure he's ever seen Lauren so . . . *insane.* "Okay, fine, just the comb. Look. I'm putting down the hair gel."

As Craig runs the comb through Killian's hair, Lauren stuffs the tube of hair gel into the pocket of her apron.

On the drive over to Pemberley, Lauren tries to conceal her nervousness by singing along to a Beatles song on the radio. Killian says nothing, asks one question: "How will I find you afterwards?"

"We're going to be in the library," Lauren says.

"Is it far away?"

"Nope. It's across the hall about two doors down from where you'll be. It's very close."

"Good. I just wanted to make sure you would be close by."

"I'm going to be very close by, I promise."

Lauren realizes now that Killian, too, is nervous.

They pull into the parking lot, climb out of the car, and head slowly toward the kindergarten classrooms. Suddenly, Killian says, "Fuckly."

"What?"

"Fuckly," he repeats, and points at a sign that says "Faculty."

Thank God, Lauren thinks. *I thought he was pissed off about the process and cursing me out.*

· · ·

Pemberley begins the evaluation with a clever, nasty trick.

Lauren and Killian enter the library. Dana and Gail greet them. Dana says hello, then asks each parent to fill out a nametag, which are laid out on a table. Lauren leans over the table and begins writing her name. As she is writing, she notices out of the corner of her eye that Gail has grabbed Killian's hand and is whisking him away.

"Bye, Killian," Lauren says. "See you in an hour."

But he's gone.

In a few minutes, after the kids have all been taken from the room, Reese, the head of Pemberley School, comes in and explains about the nametag diversionary tactic.

"Look, we have the technology here to print out lovely nametags in colorful fonts, but we do it this way so you have something to do while we take your kids," she says. "Otherwise, believe me, we wouldn't get half of them in there. At least not without a fight."

After slightly less than an hour of questions the kids return. They march in, all wearing nametags. Lauren practically jogs over to Killian. "Hey, you got a nametag," she says.

"Yep. We had to find them ourselves."

"What else did you guys do?"

"Nothing."

"Nothing? Come on. What did you do?"

Killian shrugs. "I'm not going to tell you."

I Don't *Wanna*

On Thursday and Friday, Katie Miller guards what she says to her daughter Alex. She does not want to create any sense of anxiety, but at the same time she wants Alex to look forward to her Saturday morning "play date" at Hunsford.

"I want her to be aware of it. In a fun way," she tells Trina D'Angelo on the phone. "I don't want to make a big deal about it."

"You want her to be prepared, that's all," Trina says.

"Correct. No surprises. I think after Evergreen, she'll be fine. She had such a good time there. I've been telling her it'll be basically the same thing." Katie sighs. "Trina, this is so draining."

"Honey, she will kill at Hunsford. Afterwards, you'll write a lovely letter. And then all we have to do is distract ourselves for three fucking months while we wait for the mail to come."

"That is the worst part, I swear."

"Why do we have to wait so long? Why can't they let you know like in two weeks?"

"When I rule the world," Katie says, "I will change that."

•   •   •

"Let's try to make this like any other Saturday morning," Katie says to Miles over coffee. It is just after seven o'clock.

Hunched over the sports section, her husband grunts, scratches the stubble on his cheek. He yawns. "You want me to take her to breakfast?"

"I think so, yeah. Keep it normal. You take her to breakfast, I'll go to the bank with Nicky. Just be back no later than nine forty-five. Her interview is at ten-twenty."

Miles nods. Katie refills his cup, adds a splash to hers, starts to drink, sighs, dumps the coffee into the sink.

"I'm a teeny bit nervous," she says.

"No, really?" Miles says, not looking up from the paper.

"Just a tad," Katie says on her way out of the room.

. . .

It takes longer than Katie expects at the bank. She has discovered inconsistencies in her account, possibly forgery. Opening a new account, transferring funds, filling out forms, and dealing with two-year-old Nick, who was not thrilled being dragged away from his favorite Saturday morning cartoon, takes more time and causes more tension than she had anticipated. When she pulls into the driveway with her account settled and Nick in tow, it is nearly ten. She is eager to get to Hunsford. Entering the living room, she is surprised to find Alex camped in front of the television, still in her pajamas. Inexplicably, Miles has not gotten her ready for the interview.

"Hey, kiddo, how was breakfast with Daddy?"

"Good."

"Great." Katie claps her hands. "Okay. Time to get dressed. We have to go."

Alex leans back on her elbows, cranes her neck up toward Katie. "Mom, I've changed my mind. I'm not going to Hunsford."

Katie grabs the remote and clicks off the TV. "Of course we're going. Now come on, we don't want to be late."

"I told you. I'm not going."

And then as if she hadn't made herself completely clear, Alex repeats, "I'm not going to that school."

From somewhere deep inside, Katie summons an entire reservoir of perkiness and with her cheeks puffed out grotesquely says, "But, honey, we accepted the invitation. They invited us and we said we were gonna come . . ."

Here it comes. The whining. A high-gear, pedal-down, head-crunching *whirrr* straight out of a power drill.

"I don't *wanna* go. I don't *wanna*, I don't *wanna*, I don't *wanna*—"

I'm dying, Katie says to herself. *I'm gonna die right here, right now.*

"I don't WANNA."

I'm in hell.

Come on, come on. Get ahold of yourself. Okay. Now . . .

What am I gonna do?

I can't believe this is happening. Of all the times and of all the places . . . Think. Think.

SHIT! WHERE ARE MY PARENTING TOOLS RIGHT NOW? SHITTTTT!!!

"I am not going."

Ice. Creepy as that little kid from *The Ring.*

Through gritted teeth, low, inaudibly, Katie hisses back, "The fuck you're not."

Do not do this.

Katie feels herself starting to sweat. She looks at her daughter, glances at the time, 10:04, and she just wants to rip the pajamas off her, throw her clothes on, and shove her into the car seat.

"MILES!"

She has never heard herself scream that loudly or that frantically.

"*HELP!*"

As if out of a mist, he appears. He is wearing a white T-shirt, shorts, and flip-flops. His hair is a fright. He looks as if he's just stepped out of a wind. He is holding the latest copy of *Rolling Stone*.

"Yeah?"

"I DON'T WANNA GO TO HUNSFORD." Daring them now. Alex's face reads, "Make me."

Katie's pulse is pounding in her head like a jackhammer. She can barely hear herself speak.

"Miles, what do we do? We have to be there in five minutes. *What do we do?*"

His eyes scan the living room, from his daughter, sitting defiantly on the living room floor, to his wife, standing unsteadily in front of the couch, her eyes red with panic. His knees creak as he bends down, eye to eye with Alex.

"Will you go to Hunsford if I take you? Just you and me?"

A two-second hold that feels like twenty minutes.

"Yes," Alex says.

"Let me get your clothes," Katie says, sprinting out of the room.

She is in Alex's room in less than a heartbeat, her hands reaching for the drawstring pants. But where is the drawstring? Great. Disappeared somewhere inside the waistband.

"Aw hell," Katie says, her voice deepening into disaster register. She flings the pants into the corner, whips open Alex's dresser, and pulls out a pair of jeans. This will do. They'll have to. It is no longer about the outfit. It is only about getting her there in one piece, in some semblance of a cooperative mood. Katie races back into the living room. With lightning speed, she hoists the pajama tops over her daughter's head, wrestles the blue top on. PJ bottoms off, jeans on, shoes on, tied, and let's go!

And they are gone, her daughter in an outfit that is actually cute, and her husband, the last-second replacement, off to Hunsford, the school of her dreams, looking as if he's just come in from washing the car.

"I can't believe this," she says aloud. "This is not happening. I cannot sit here for two hours."

She checks the flyer on the bulletin board in the kitchen and sees that, thankfully, Nick has a gym class scheduled at ten-thirty. They are in the SUV in seconds, he stuffed into the car seat, looking confused, she driving, her hands gripping the steering wheel in a state of shock. Ten minutes later, she settles Nick into class, walks outside, and calls Miles on her cell.

"*Well?*"

"It's okay," Miles says.

"Did she separate?"

"No problem. She wouldn't even say good-bye to me."

Katie is dying another death. She should be at Hunsford with Alex. Seeing it through. It's the least she deserves. This has been her cause, her purpose. All the time, emotion, and angst she has expended. The nightmare vomit dream. All of it. All leading up to this day, this moment, and she is not even there. She feels abandoned.

"Tell me," she says.

"We get there, we're a little late, but it's fine. This teacher comes over, Cary or something, or Amy, I don't remember her name. Anyway, she says, 'Hi, Alex, will you come with me?' Alex says, 'Sure,' and that was it. She starts to go off with her. I say, 'Aren't you going to say good-bye to me?' She says, 'No.' I say, 'Okay, then blow me a kiss. One little kiss.' She says, 'No,' and they go off."

"Great. They must think she's like the wildest little bitch in the world."

Miles says nothing. Katie pictures him sitting at Hunsford, so out of place. She starts to ask if he feels uncomfortable, thinks better of it. At least Alex is there. And she seems all right.

"I have to do something to keep my mind off this. But call me."

"I will."

"Or I'll call you."

"Either way."

Katie flips her cell closed. She steps back inside the kids' gym, catches Nick's eye, fastens on a smile, and waves excitedly, as if he'd just won a gold medal.

•   •   •

They met back at home at noon. Katie, desperate for details, begged for the morning's play-by-play. Miles, doing the best he could, which is not much because he is both a guy and *Miles*, remembered that when it was over, the teachers brought the parents into the classroom. Alex climbed into his lap and he read her a couple of books. He said he was there for a couple of minutes, tops.

Katie tried to pump Alex for information. She said she had a pretty good time. Katie asked her what kind of projects she did. Alex said they did Play-Doh and she made three red hearts. Then they had her draw a horse. Katie laughed. She knew that Alex had never drawn a horse in her life. Alex slammed her thumb into her mouth and curled up on the couch and within a few minutes she was asleep.

Well, as long as she didn't hate Hunsford, Katie thought.

Katie sat on the couch next to her sleeping daughter and stroked her hair. She thought about something a friend had told her. She said that you should ask your kid for her opinion. Make them a part of the process. Katie smiled, recalling an expression she'd heard from another mom: "You have your say, but you don't get your way."

"Sorry, honey," she whispered to Alex. "You don't get your say about picking your school. High school, yes. College, yes. Kindergarten, no. This is all about me, sweetheart."

The truth was that while Alex was being interviewed, or tested, or whatever they call it at Hunsford, Katie was doing something else. Yes, she did all those errands. She needed to divert her attention. Needed to keep busy. But that's not really what Katie did.

What she really did was pray.

The whole time. She just prayed. She prayed to God.

"Please, God," she prayed, slowly caressing her sleeping daughter's hair, "please let them love her."

CHAPTER EIGHT

Decision

I've never heard no in my life. I'm not gonna take no from you.

—a prospective parent to a private school director of admissions

Parents should know this: they are their own worst enemies.

—a private school director of admissions

The Four Questions

Do first-choice letters matter?

In the corner of Starbucks, seated in a pair of high-backed armchairs, twin thrones, Trina D'Angelo and Katie Miller pass a saucer back and forth containing the crumbled remains of a blueberry muffin and discuss first-choice letters. Trina has just revealed to Katie that she has fallen in love with St. Mary's Christian, an off-the-radar Catholic school that is half the cost of Meryton. It is also halfway across town. Still, St. Mary's has now emerged as Trina's first choice.

"Are you going to write them a first-choice letter?" Katie asks.

"I did. But there's a problem." Trina wraps her hands around her coffee cup and stares into it. "I also wrote one to Meryton."

Katie dips her head and shakes it slowly.

"I know, I know, I shouldn't have," Trina says. "When I wrote the letter to Meryton, I meant it. But that was five months ago. Meryton was my first choice then. Did I do a terrible thing?"

• • •

Of course, there are worse transgressions in life than sending out multiple first-choice letters, although none come to mind. Unfortunately, the kindergarten application process can make our most well-meaning and incorruptible citizens stoop to bizarre (remember the five-foot self-standing photograph?) and even unethical behavior. The first-choice letter, once a reliable addendum to the application, has plummeted in value, correlating to the rise in parents' stress levels.

"I used to value first-choice letters," said Edgar Mantle, head of Evergreen School. "But a few years ago I got a letter that began, 'Pemberley is far and away our first choice.' I called Pemberley and found out they got the same letter from the same family that began, 'Evergreen is far and away our first choice.' That's when I stopped taking first-choice letters seriously."

"It's great for a family to write a first-choice letter, but I tend to rely more on the preschool director's word," MK, admissions director at New York's prestigious Longbourne School, said.

DJ, head of one of the country's top private schools, said, "We look at first-choice letters with a grain of salt because we've been burned. Every school has. Many times we'd get a first-choice letter, we'd say yes, then the family says no. Those stories are kind of legendary. A family wrote six first-choice letters one year and then got nailed on it. It's to the point that if I get a first-choice letter I'll always confirm it with the preschool."

Still, it doesn't hurt to write a first-choice letter.

Unless you write more than one.

•   •   •

Do admissions directors talk to each other?

I had always assumed that admissions directors talked, but because of the classified nature of the process—the closed-door secrecy in which decisions were made—I figured that they talked after they'd mailed out their acceptance letters and they'd received all of their replies. I imagined their conversations to be in the nature of postmortems at conferences over coffee: "Yes, this was a tough year, so many girls." "I know. And we had so many siblings. More tea?" My images were quaint, genteel, formal.

The thought that admissions directors might speak to each other *during* the process and engage in conversation that might affect their decision-making didn't occur to me until I spoke to a couple of prospective parents who asked, "Do you think they compare notes, talk about who's applying where? Do you think they make deals?"

I tried to envision admissions directors as backroom wheeler-dealers or baseball general managers: "I'll trade you the Spielberg kid for the black math genius and a child to be named later."

I couldn't picture it. But I had to ask. And I found out that my crazy scenario wasn't all that far off.

•   •   •

"We share information. We do. We talk. All the time."

Edgar Mantle squirmed in his chair. His confession had made him uncomfortable, as if he'd just ratted out his friends. It turns out he had plenty of corroboration.

"Everybody talks to everybody, on every level, all the way up to senior year of high school," an educational consultant said. "We all know it."

MK, Longbourne's director of admissions, after confirming that all identities in this book would be anonymous, said, "We do talk. Of course, everybody travels in a slightly different circle. For me, I have a couple of people, close friends in the business . . . I call and talk with them. We will talk about certain things, certain families. We're very honest. We share information. We keep each other in the loop. I'd say we're *collegial*."

"My attitude is maybe I can help place the families that don't get in," Dana Optt said. "I talk with most of the admissions directors. We compare lists. We know who the hot families are and which schools have taken them. It's just the way it's done."

Nan F., director of admissions at the prestigious Darcy School, openly, but gingerly, described how she shares information.

"Let me say first that we care about kids, all of us, at least the directors I know and work closely with: Brianna at Hunsford, Elizabeth at Meryton, and Dana at Pemberley. We work hard to make sure that kids don't get shut out. When we see a wonderful family with a wonderful kid but there is no space at their first-choice school, by God, we will help you. You may not get into the school you wanted, but we'll find a good place for you. We talk the day before the letters go out, or even before that, to see who we're all accepting.

"It's not like the New York thing that's, 'Oh, they're going to go there so let's not accept them.' It's more like, 'Oh, you are going to take them? Well, we love them, too, so we'll take them also and they can choose for themselves.'

"But cross-acceptances don't usually turn out that way. I am always relieved when somebody I loved who I couldn't take ends up getting into Meryton or Pemberley or wherever. There is ongoing chatter about this.

"We all run our admit list, our waitlist, and the people we're definitely not going to take by each other. We're looking for common ground. So we know ahead of time. We call each other. I don't think it dramatically influences the decisions that we have already made, but psychologically you may be sort of pleased that yes, these people that we really liked are getting in somewhere. You also may be distressed to learn that nobody is taking a particular child and you aren't either.

"Here's an example of how it can work. Two years ago, we happened to have an opening in fourth grade. I called Brianna, Dana, and Elizabeth and I told them, 'We've had all these applications and none of them are going to work.' Elizabeth said, 'I have this fabulous family who applied and no room.' So I took her interview notes, took all her records, everything. I had never met the family. They never applied here. I talked to them on the phone. They came for a visit, I ended up accepting the kid, and it's been fine. This scenario has happened in every grade, including kindergarten. We have this camaraderie. We help each other.

"I trust these women and they trust me. They're absolutely my favorite people in this business. I feel very much on the same wavelength with them. And because we have the kids' interests at heart, I think it's valuable to have a collegial relationship with them. Why not? It's all for the sake of the kids."

·　　·　　·

Do siblings automatically get in?

According to virtually everyone I spoke to, always. Well, almost always. Being a well-adjusted, reasonably bright younger brother or sister will pretty much guarantee a spot in your older sibling's school. In fact, my anecdotal research brought me to the conclusion that in most private schools a sib would have to indicate nearly off-the-chart behavioral or learning issues in order not to be admitted.

"Sometimes we have to turn siblings away," an admissions director said. "It's the hardest thing I do. For about two weeks in January I meet with families who have siblings I'm not going to admit. That is the worst. Trying to explain why; trying to be honest and diplomatic at the same time, tiptoeing around some of the most powerful people in town. Not easy."

Dana Optt explained her specific approach at Pemberley. "The first thing I do every year is plug in faculty, alumni kids, and siblings. I see them in January. I have everything in a grid: their birthdays, their personalities, preschools, parents' occupations, and the overall energy of the class. From there I do a very comprehensive overview. I was talking to our head yesterday, going through this, and I said, 'I've been looking very carefully at the girls who have May and June birthdays. We have to pick a couple of them to mix with these siblings. And I need an artistic boy who's not athletic. I actually need a couple of those. We've got too many jocks.' It is all about the makeup of the class. You can be the most amazing boy, sitting right on top of the pile, you're the next mad genius who's going to come to Pemberley, and I'll say, 'Shoot. All the siblings took the July birthdays. I can't take this kid.' Social skills and maturity are very key factors here. Then I sit with my committee and we look at all the siblings again. We consider each kid's energy. You don't want a class that's so high-energy they're impossible to control. And you don't want a class that's so laid-back and lethargic that you fall asleep every morning at ten. What I'm getting at is that I try to keep the focus on the kids the whole time."

·   ·   ·

> More money than God. That's the going rate.
> Less than that may not help.
>
> —*an educational consultant*

Do people buy their way in?

Invariably, this question turned admissions directors and school heads into a collection of mutes and mimes. The variety of nonverbal responses I received included shrugs, smiles both wide and thin, laughs ranging from cackles to guffaws, deep reddening of cheeks, violent clearing of throats, shaking of heads, impatient and irritated sighs, exhalations of air weak and strong, scratching of chins and scalps, and a symphony of sounds and syllables such as "Hmm," "Ooh," and "Argh." One director of admissions did answer in a complete sentence. She said, "I'm not going to go there."

Interestingly, no one said no.

When it comes to the question of money, what matters most, as in most things, is how the sensitive subject is framed.

"We weren't sure how to approach the money issue on the application," Lauren Pernice said. "You can't blatantly say, 'We will give you money.' That sounds crass. Ultimately we decided not to address it at all and just have somebody we know at the school say that we can be counted on to give generously."

Lauren has articulated by far the most acceptable approach. As an educational consultant said, "I believe, no, I *know*, that if you have someone going to bat for you, someone with clout, it will work. Powerful people get in. Powerful people with a lot of money get in. And powerful people who know powerful people with money get in. If I tell a school that this is a great family who will be generous with their time and resources, it will help. A lot."

In other words, as an admissions director said, "Bill Gates's kid is gonna get in. Period."

The most famous example of attempting to buy one's way in occurred in 2002 when Manhattan-based mutual fund manager Jack Grubman attempted to manipulate a million dollars' worth of AT&T stock in order to get his twins into the 92nd Street Y preschool, a prime feeder into New York's elite kindergartens. Grubman got caught. His twins have since been condemned to public school, their lives now apparently doomed.

It's safe to assume that if Grubman hadn't gotten caught, he would've gotten in. Bill Gates's fame and well-documented generosity and Grubman's assessment that a million dollars would buy him two spots at the 92nd Street Y beg the question: if you can buy your way in, what is the going rate?

"I heard a kid got into Meryton last year because the dad set up an endowment," Trina D'Angelo said. "We're talking more money than God. If you're not in that ballpark, you're screwed."

I have heard a litany of stories, some no doubt apocryphal, in which others, monetary mortals, have tried and failed. A wealthy businessman desperate to secure a kindergarten spot for his daughter in a prestigious parochial school privately approached the director of admissions and asked if there was anything in particular she needed at the school.

"What's at the top of your wish list?" he asked.

"We would really love a new stained-glass window," she said.

Within a week, workers and artisans were dispatched, and in a few months a new stained-glass window was installed at the preschool, costing upwards of $25,000. It wasn't enough. His daughter didn't get in.

Another man began writing an annual $5,000 check to a prestigious private school beginning the week his child was born.

Again not enough. His child was refused.

But another woman was told in her interview that if she wanted a spot for her daughter, she needed to take out her checkbook and write a check for $10,000 right then.

"That's how much a kindergarten spot costs today," the interviewer told her.

"I'm not sure I'm willing to do that," the woman said.

"That's fine," the interviewer said. "Plenty of people are."

The woman wrote the check. Her child got in.

I have seen cases firsthand in which children of families with more money than God have leapfrogged over the rest of the pack and landed firmly in the center of incoming kindergarten classes. Many private schools operate on a deficit; they rely on fund-raising or donations from families within or connected to their community to make up the difference. As the cost of living soars, parents who willingly open their wallets, especially when it comes to major expenses, are always in demand. But having more money than God doesn't necessarily mean an eagerness to part with it.

"Every acceptance is a leap of faith for both the family and the school," said Nan F., director of admissions at the Darcy School. "It's hard but I know we're on firm ground if we refuse a kid who's really bad, a clear 1, even if the family is high-profile. I can't tell you how many times someone will pledge a million dollars to our building campaign and end up not paying it off. And especially with an elementary school, there is no philanthropic record for most families. I'm sure it's tempting for many schools to sweep everything under the rug because Daddy is going to give a million dollars. But no one wants to deal with a child who is miserable. I would hope that no school would take a child who they just knew was going to be a failure, even if it meant sustaining him for a while so they could use some of Daddy's money."

Despite Nan's hopes, I heard several stories of schools accepting kids just for the money. Dana Optt offered this example:

"I know a case in which a school, not Pemberley, took the most obnoxious woman I have ever met who has a kid with severe learning issues. I'm like, 'Okay, that one's clear. It's all about money.' I called my friend, the admissions director, and I said, 'You're kidding me.'

"She said, 'Dana, this is known as Board Power. My hands are tied.'"

In the end, allowing a family to buy a spot in kindergarten is not without risk. Everything comes with a price tag; a family's generosity rarely arrives without strings. Even if the strings are invisible to the naked eye, the school officials and the family know they are there, waiting to be yanked at any time.

"One thing that's happening now, unique to this time, is that parents are *buying* a school and everything that goes with it: the amenities, philosophy, reputation, everything," Nan F. said. "The private school population has changed. The parents are often people who have grown up going to public schools, who would actually prefer to send their kids to public school, but who can't or won't because of what they perceive as the problems with public school education. These people are paying $20,000 a year *plus* for kindergarten and they expect a lot for their money. It's a whole different mentality and it has put a ton of pressure on the schools. If you're spending twenty grand a year minimum, you want your kid to be the smartest in the class, the best athlete, the best artist, and ultimately to get into the best college. Parents of kindergarten kids have become consumers. They want the biggest bang for their buck. If the school doesn't deliver, especially if they are major contributors, they will let the school know. Big time."

Who Gets In

"When we decide which kids we're gonna take, it works like this."

Edgar Mantle waves his bear-sized hand over his head as if he's about to shake an invisible tambourine.

"Connie, the director of admissions, the kindergarten teachers, and I sit around the conference table. All our applications are complete. The interview has happened, the child visit has happened, all the reports are in, and all the support letters are attached. This is in late February, I think. Time tends to blur."

He laughs suddenly, which disintegrates into a worrying cough. He takes a deep breath, steadies himself, scratches his scalp.

"Prior to this, we've taken about two weeks, very intense time, when we have to read all the files. So we sit down in the conference room and we go. Everybody has their numbers ready. Now, we have a form for the kids as well. Same thing as the parent form, a kind of checklist, ranked from 1 to 3. The form is really just to try to help the teachers organize their think-ing. That way at the end of the visit, they can write something down about each kid."

Edgar pats his head, this time leaving his palm resting on the top of his head like a skullcap. "We look at the red flags first. The 1s. A kid gets a 1 from the teachers, you have to follow that up, take a look at the child's application and nursery school re-port and all that. What gets you a 1? If a child can't participate, if a child doesn't let go of a parent, if a child has huge separation issues, if a child smacks a teacher or a kid, if a child takes a bite out of me. Then again, maybe the kid knows something."

Edgar bellows out a roar, then stops on a dime.

"We insist that teachers don't look at a file before a visit. We don't want to prejudice them in any way. For the most part, kids want to fit in. That is their natural instinct. You look for that. Kids who want to stand out, who are trying to be noticed . . . that's a potential red flag. Kids don't want to be known as different."

Edgar pauses, folds his hands on his desk. "When we start, we go around the table and write down all the numbers. Connie is the de facto scribe, recording secretary, whatever you want to call it. A child who gets straight 3s is obviously right for the school. That's not one we need to talk about. But then it's 'Gee, look at this. Two 3s and two 1s. This might be worth a conversa-tion.' We go back and forth, back and forth. There could be many rounds of talking about particular kids or families. You keep making the pot smaller. It's a constant honing-down process."

•   •   •

Dana Optt begins making her decisions after each Saturday visit, beginning in early January. "I start weeding out right then.

You just know some things immediately. You certainly know for whom this is the wrong school, the wrong setting. You ask, 'Is this child going to struggle? Are we setting up this child to fail?' I won't put a child, or a family, or Pemberley through that. It's not fair. It's not right."

Dana's process involves creating three piles: one for children she likes, one for those on the fence, one for those who are definite *no's*. "I go through everything: what the preschool teachers wrote, what the kindergarten teachers wrote after the child visit, and my interview sheets. Then I weed the piles further: *This is a phenomenal kid, teachers love the kid, did great at his visit* or *I think the parent will be a nightmare. She asked if we teach algebra in kindergarten.* Okay, next."

In a typical season, Pemberley will receive in excess of three hundred applications. "I can easily weed out a hundred to a hundred fifty right away," Dana said. "You watch and you just know. There are obvious indicators. Transitioning, for example. In many typical kindergartens, you stay with the same teacher all day in the same room. Here you've got a big campus. You're going to go to PE, then to the music room, and so forth. You could be a really bright kid but you may have difficulty with transitions. You can tell who is capable of that kind of atmosphere. Even if you might be great by second or third grade, if I stress you out for two years, to me that's not the right thing. People say their kid will grow into it. I say I will have ruined them. It's the wrong thing to do."

Despite pedigree, power, money, or all three, there are certain kids whom Dana will just not admit. Next to siblings, these are her most agonizing decisions, resulting in her most difficult conversations. "I can't help it," Dana said, her voice tinged with agony. "These kids just don't belong here."

This season, there was a powerful guy. Dana met with the family three times. She *tried*. But there was no way. She spoke at length to the preschool, evaluated the child personally.

"The kid refused to go with me," she said. "The mother said to the kid, 'Now, honey, we flew all the way back from the south of France to meet Dana.'"

The kid looked up at Dana. "I don't like you."

"I don't blame you," Dana said. "You're probably exhausted."

"Yeah. And I'm not doing anything you tell me."

"It doesn't sound like it's his day," Dana said to the mother. "Why don't you take him to the playground and see if he's ready in a little while. If not, bring him back next week."

"He never acts like this," the mother said.

She brought him back the following Saturday. The kid glared at Dana and said, "I'm still not doing anything you say. Unless you give me an electronic toy."

"I bet your mom will give you anything," Dana said. "You come with me, you do what I say, and I guarantee you will get an electronic toy, maybe two."

Maybe she'll give me something, too, Dana thought. *Work with me, buddy, I need a new laptop.*

But there was nothing Dana could do. The kid was, in her words, "a disaster."

"I'm sorry," she said to the father. "I really am."

"You don't understand," he said. "We're used to winning."

The phrase rattled around in Dana's brain for two straight weeks.

We're used to winning.

"It's stunning to me," she said. "We're talking about kindergarten. And what's right for a child."

But all this powerful guy knew was that he'd lost.

• • •

Mᴋ, director of admissions at the Longbourne School in New York, begins at the end. "I have two waitlists: a high waitlist and a regular waitlist. I don't publicize that, though." A pause. "You don't know which waitlist you're on. In a very brutal system I try to be as gentle as possible. So I have four categories—admit, high waitlist, regular waitlist, and deny—but only three are public."

"I don't do a false waitlist," Dana Optt said. "I put ten boys and ten girls on one waitlist and that's it. People have no idea how I've struggled. Some of the people on the waitlist were on and off the accept list fifteen times. And I agonize over the letter. I always think I've written a sensitive letter but every year I go over what I wrote the previous year and I ask myself, 'Is there a better way to say this?' There is no good way to say no. The accept letter is a breeze. *Hello, this is Pemberley, you're in.* Whatever. All I have to say is *yes.* And the waitlist letter isn't too bad. We are one of the few schools that turn you down. Mcryton, Darcy, and Hunsford put everybody on a false waitlist. I know it's a hard pill to swallow, but I'd rather just turn you down, period. I think it's unfair to have people waiting, thinking, hoping that it might happen when the school knows it won't. I believe it's much better to say, 'This is not going to happen. Let's focus on the other possibilities.' As hard as that is, it's more humane."

• • •

Among the families Dana Optt will reject are Howard and Lionel, the two charming, funny, successful gay men she met at the Private School Expo who adopted Justin, the adorable African-American boy. Lionel, the stay-at-home dad, fussed over the application as if it were a master's thesis, calling Dana for moral support before he was able to relinquish the paperwork and hand it in.

"How did we do on the essay?" Lionel asked her on the phone a week after submitting their application.

"For God's sake, it was fine," Dana said.

"Howard wrote it. I think he made us all sound shallow."

"It was *fine*."

"I thought he came off as an Asian Paris Hilton."

"You know what? You need to go back to work. You're driving yourself nuts."

"Wish I could. This parenting gig is tough. My biggest fear is that when Justin grows up, he's going to call his memoir *Daddies Dearest*."

Dana looked forward to their interview. She was counting on them to provide her with much-needed comic relief from the wanton anxiety and brazen narcissism that made up many of the other interviews. She was not disappointed. Their interview was the most enjoyable hour and fifteen minutes she would spend the entire season. It was by turns hilarious, emotional, and inspirational. Howard and Lionel were brutally honest about their inadequacies as parents and the unanticipated daily challenges and frustrations of fatherhood. Dana told them how much she admired them. She was rooting for them, she said, pulling hard for Justin. She couldn't reveal it to them then, but she knew that if Justin performed even marginally well on his Saturday assessment, they were an easy admit, a no-brainer.

Five minutes into Justin's Saturday visit, Dana's heart sank. She saw immediately that Justin was a child with extreme attention and language processing issues. He was completely unfocused, incapable of participating in even one activity. She had observed kids like Justin before, many of whom were children of severely drug-addicted mothers, Justin's behavior identified him as a classic case. After his disastrous Saturday visit, she pulled out his preschool report. The director of his nursery school had written a recommendation that was guarded and hesitant, couched in language that indicated an awareness of Justin's issues without directly naming them. Dana thought back to their interview. Clearly, Howard and Lionel had no idea how badly Justin needed help. As for admitting him to Pemberley, Dana had no choice. She filled out his evaluation form, condemning him to the reject pile.

• • •

The day after the letters go out, Dana sits at her computer going through her e-mails, of which there are more than two hundred. Her incoming mail clicks and she sees a message from Lionel.

"We are so disappointed that there was no space at Pemberley for Justin. I have to say that we're not surprised. We know from the 'park bench' buzz that this was an extremely competitive year, even more so than usual. And since everyone wants Pemberley, well, we can do the math. Again, Dana, thank you for considering Justin (and us) and it was a pleasure getting to know you. Fondly, Howard and Lionel."

Dana finds Howard and Lionel's e-mail heartbreaking. She reads it again, then dials their number. She gets Lionel's voice on their voice mail. She leaves a short message, saying only, "This is Dana. After you receive your letters from the other schools, if you'd be interested in hearing some feedback, give me a call."

Lionel calls back in less than five minutes.

"We didn't get in anywhere," he says.

"Unfortunately, I'm not surprised," Dana says.

"Dana, I have to tell you something. Two weeks ago, our preschool told us that Justin needs to be evaluated."

Dana feels sudden, emphatic relief. "I am really glad to hear that. Lionel, you and Howard have to know that there are things you can do right now to allow Justin to have a very successful school experience. And thankfully, you are in a position where financially you can provide the best—"

"Money is no object. We will spend whatever it takes to help him."

"There is nothing like early intervention in a case like his," Dana says. "Look, he has a lot of strengths."

"We are royally pissed at the preschool," Lionel says. "They waited until two weeks before the letters went out to tell us."

"I don't understand that. Maybe they wanted to be sure."

Lionel says nothing.

"Again, the important thing is it's early," Dana says. "Do you need some names?"

"We already have an appointment."

"You guys move fast."

"It's our kid," Lionel says.

"After you have the evaluation, call me. I can be helpful in directing you to some appropriate schools and I can recommend some really good ed therapists to work with."

Lionel's voice cracks. "Thank you."

"Call me."

"I will."

"Lionel, this is not going to be easy. You have to be prepared for some rocky times."

"Little different than what we signed up for."

"It always is."

Gifted and Talented

"We are *done*." Poised at the tip of her couch in her Upper East Side apartment, Shea Cohen sings the last word, holds the note for an improbable five seconds. "Yesterday was Liam's last interview."

Shea scoops a handful of unsalted peanuts into her mouth from an ornate glass dish, nods, and says through munching, "It was a disaster. The worst. For some reason, everyone I know in New York happened to be sitting in the admissions office watching us being interviewed. The woman who was interviewing us was not very nice. I made the mistake of . . . Well, this is really bad."

Another swipe of nuts. This time accompanied by her lop-sided grin. "I wanted to tell her something and I called her the name of an admissions director from another school. I couldn't believe it. I was like, 'I'm so sorry. Of course I know your name. I didn't mean to refer to you as . . .' Wow. That was *terrible*. Then the topper is Liam came in and he was completely disheveled. He didn't even look like him. I don't know what he was doing. His hair was a big mess, his clothes were all schlumpy, he looked like hell. In the background, I heard this woman I know, a soon-to-be-ex-friend, say, 'You'd think they'd at least have him look nice for the interview.' Nothing like being interviewed in front of all your peers who see your kid look like he's just come out of a hurricane and you insult the director of admissions by calling her a different name. It was a private school catastrophe."

Shea nudges the bowl of nuts away, just out of reach.

"Honestly, at this point, I'm sort of bored with the whole thing. I think I'm more curious about where other people's kids are going than I am about where Liam is going to end up. He'll have his place. He'll have a spot in a very good school, I'm sure of that. So, yeah, I'm tired of it all. However, there is a sort of curveball. There are a few public schools in the city, one or two on the West Side and a couple downtown, who house within their elementary school something called a gifted and talented program. It's almost like a separate school within a school. The one nearest us, Netherfield, is in fact its own independent school. You have to apply to get in. You have to take the Stanford-Binet test, which is an IQ test. If he scores like a 97 or above on that, they invite you to tour the school, then they interview you, and you have an on-site. It's very competitive. I think they take eighteen kids."

Shea wipes her hands on her jeans, twists open a bottle of Evian. "Liam took the Stanford-Binet, scored well, and we're applying to Netherfield, too."

She takes a swig from the bottle. "This is purely an academic program. I mean, pretty much. They have PE and music and the arts, but because it's part of the public school system, those programs really can't compete with what you're going to get at Longbourne. The advantages are, number one, academically, Netherfield is incredible. The stuff I saw kids doing in kindergarten was amazing. Number two, it's free. As in not twenty-five grand a year. All Liam has is one more group thing at Netherfield and that is it. He loved it, by the way, had a great time. He's actually kind of sad that the process is over. Last night he said to me, 'Is that it? I'm not going to any more schools?' I said, 'You're done. You want to go to any more, you can go with your own children.'"

·   ·   ·

The decisions arrive in the mail a week later. Out of the seven schools the Cohens applied to, Liam is accepted at two, Longbourne and one other, rejected at three, and waitlisted at two, including Netherfield. In terms of the New York City private school game, they have hit a home run.

"So it's Longbourne," Shea says. "It's funny. Donald and I

both feel that no school is perfect. We love the school and Liam's best friend is going so that's a big plus. But the caliber of kids there strikes me as just a level below some of the other schools. There are a lot of bright kids there, don't get me wrong, but I think Liam will really stand out. I think he'll shine. And since he's not an athlete, he needs to find his place. Our biggest hesitation is Netherfield. If need be, I think we'd forgo a deposit. It is such a good program. I'm not holding out tons of hope for that, though, because it's very tough. But we did well. This is a very competitive market and this was an extremely tough year. It really was all about Liam. We have no connections. We're not big donors. He's a good kid. He did a great job. So . . . Longbourne."

Shea says it slowly. Trying it on for size. "Unless something else materializes between now and May first. That's when we're on the hook for the whole tuition. Look, I feel very lucky. We got into two schools. I know several people who got shut out. Didn't get in anywhere. Or they got waitlisted everywhere. Or they only got into their last choice, a school about which they said, 'I would never send my kid there,' and now that's their only choice. At least we have choices."

Board Power

Thanks to her friend Susan, Lauren Pernice found herself obsessed with the math.

"Susan keeps telling me not to dwell on the numbers because the numbers are inflated," Lauren murmured in a monotone. "According to her, you knock out twenty to thirty families right away and an equal number of kids because they're just not appropriate. The result is a kind of fuzzy math because the same people apply to the same schools. Therefore, the applicant pool becomes somewhat diluted. And so I'm doing the dishes or something and my mind wanders . . . *If there are three hundred applicants and fifty are eliminated because of family and another twenty-five are siblings, we're down to two hundred twenty-five. Many of those prefer Darcy or Meryton or some other school, thus reducing the applicant pool perhaps another, I don't know, hundred or so. Now we're down to a hundred and twenty-five. Okay, not great, but better odds than three hundred for twenty spots.*"

Lauren sighed. "This is ridiculous. It just speaks to how irrationally important getting into Pemberley has become to us. It's insane how much time it takes up and how it detracts from your *life.*"

Lauren sank into the middle of the overstuffed sofa in the family room. She gazed at the hill of Killian's toys tucked into the corner of the room, a castle made of Legos, a set of plastic golf clubs, a teetering pile of board games. She lowered her freshly coiffed hairdo into the folds of her hands, then peeked up and blinked twice at the ceiling. She'd tried not to look at this process as a game, at least not at first. She insisted on going through it as aboveboard and honorably as possible.

Then she realized that she *wanted* Pemberley.

She thought about Dana and how she dealt with the onslaught of power people who would be contacting her directly or indirectly on a daily basis. People with big names or more money than God who are in her face, screaming, *"Pick me!"* Actually, Lauren figured their representatives were shouting, "Pick them!" Lauren knew that it existed that way. You'd have to be naïve to think that it didn't. She vanquished the thought, refused to join that crowd. It implied stooping to a level that she felt was somehow beneath her.

And then she realized that she was being a fool.

This *is* a game and there are rules and there are standards. There are also those things that are unspoken but understood. It is not an even playing field. And yes, bottom line, as February closed down and the calendar flipped into March, Lauren knew that she would do anything to get into Pemberley.

She called up a mom she knew at Pemberley and asked, "Do you have the list of the board of trustees?" She had looked on-line and couldn't find it. The mom read the names over the phone and Lauren typed them out while the mom was talking to her.

That night, she and Craig went over the list. Craig nodded slowly and said in a soft, matter-of-fact tone, "I've done deals with some of these people. I know three people on the list."

The first person on the list was someone Craig knew casually. He decided to try that person first, sort of feel him out. He was happy to talk to Craig. Craig was direct. He simply said, "Look, we want Pemberley. What can we do? Can we give money?"

The guy discouraged giving money up front. He said that the Pernices probably couldn't or wouldn't give enough to make an impact.

Craig called the second guy on the list. He was less helpful. He offered no advice, was somewhat curt and evasive. Craig didn't feel comfortable asking him to speak on their behalf.

Craig knew the third guy on the list the best. Before talking to him, Craig decided to hold off a day. He wanted to take some time to formulate his approach. The next morning Craig had a golf date with a friend, a guy who does in fact have more money than God. This person, Mr. Money, has a son who is applying to kindergarten next year.

This is when you know you're in a different league: Meryton, Darcy, and Pemberley have already contacted *him*. A year before he's even applying!

Mr. Money told this to Craig while they were walking up the first fairway.

And the person from Pemberley who had contacted him?

The third guy on the list.

Craig called Third Guy that night. He was very friendly. Craig never revealed the details to Lauren but she conjured up a conversation laden with implied negotiating. She imagined Third Guy thinking, *If I put in a good word for the Pernice family, then the Pernice family owes me and I will ask them to help me recruit Mr. Money.*

I scratch your back, you scratch mine, we both scratch Mr. Money's back. Everybody's itch gets scratched.

Third Guy said he would be happy to speak to Dana on behalf of the Pernices. He would make it abundantly clear that Pemberley was by far their first choice. In return Third Guy said, "You've got to volunteer and you've got to contribute financially."

It would be a Pernice team effort. Lauren promised to be a presence at Pemberley and Craig assured Third Guy that they could be counted on to provide hefty annual giving and capital campaign checks.

"I feel that if our connection gets us in, we have to pay him and Pemberley back," Lauren said. "I want to, anyway. Our goal is to be good citizens of the school, and we will be."

Third Guy called Craig a few nights later. He had met with Dana personally and communicated to her that Pemberley was their first, second, and third choice.

"I think we're in a good position," Lauren said quietly. She closed her eyes, massaged her forehead, and sank deeper into the sofa.

• • •

When Lauren Pernice picks up her mail on Wednesday, March 23, she is surprised to find among the bills and magazines a letter from Pemberley School. Not a packet, she realizes, her hands trembling, a letter. Her heart literally thumps as she tears open the envelope and reads:

Dear Lauren and Craig, Thank you for your patience concerning Killian's application to Pemberley School. Killian has been placed on the waitlist. The number of candidates to whom we would like to offer admissions far exceeds . . .

"Shit," she says aloud.

She quickly scans the rest of the letter, four paragraphs in all. The second paragraph indicates that families have until April 13 to accept *"our invitation."* The third paragraph states that Pemberley is *"very conservative in our acceptance numbers, so we typically do have the opportunity to draw a few students from our waitlist. The waitlist is unranked. We ask that you complete and return the enclosed card."*

"Great," Lauren mutters. Her stomach flips as she reads on, a closing paragraph thanking them for their participation in the Pemberley admissions process. She rereads the second paragraph, which ends by saying that Pemberley will *"extend invitations for unfilled openings as soon as possible."*

She heads into the kitchen and calls Craig on his cell.

"We're waitlisted at Pemberley," she says the moment Craig answers. "I just got the mail. They sent the letters out early."

"Huh," Craig says.

"Are you with a client?"

"Yes." A pause. "I'm surprised."

"Somehow I'm not. I actually thought we'd get on the wait-list. But expecting it and seeing it in writing—"

"I'm very surprised. I thought we'd get in," Craig says.

Lauren sighs. "Oh well. So now what?"

"We're gonna have to talk about this later," Craig says.

"Pemberley never takes anyone off the waitlist," Lauren says. "They're kind of known for that. This sucks."

"I know. Thanks for letting me know."

Lauren hangs up. Her mouth suddenly feels very dry. She opens the fridge, stares for a moment at an open bottle of chardonnay, reaches in and grabs a Snapple. She sits down at the kitchen table and reads the letter several more times, entering, as she will later describe, the first of her five stages of mourning.

• • •

"I've been through the denial, the disbelief, and the anger," Lauren tells a friend over the phone. "My first reaction was shock. I was blindsided. I didn't expect to hear until Friday."

"What are you going to do?"

"Well, I'm going to check the box and mail back the card. That's number one."

"Are you going to call Dana?"

"I'm going to have Craig do that." Lauren hesitates. "And we're certainly going to call the people we know at Pemberley."

There is a long pause. "Frankly," Lauren says, her voice blanketed now in sadness, "I'm not holding out much hope. I know people who have gotten in off the waitlist at Hunsford and Evergreen. But I don't know a single soul who's gotten in off the waitlist at Pemberley."

Lauren pauses again. A joyful child's scream punctuates the silence.

"I started this whole line of internal questioning. Second-guessing," Lauren says, her voice rising. "What did we do wrong? I should've volunteered more at Killian's preschool. I should've spoken better at the interview. I should've made Killian happier before his visit. I did about thirty minutes of this. I think I'm past that stage now."

"What stage are you in now?"

"I'm in the maybe-it-was-meant-to-be stage. You know, it's all for the best. I probably wouldn't have fit in with the parents at Pemberley, anyway. Oh well." She sighs heavily. "We haven't heard from Wickham yet, but we're not getting in. We didn't even try that hard. The silver lining, if there is one, is that our public school is supposedly very good, although whenever I check it out, I don't love it. But if Killian ends up there, so be it. It would've been so great. Kindergarten through twelfth grade covered. I *hate* thinking about going through this again in six years. I am truly dreading that. This was our way out of that."

Another long pause. Lauren's silence feels like a deep dark hole.

"This is such a lengthy emotional process," she says finally. "And how about the hope? That was the thing. For all these weeks, months, you're hanging on to this *hope*. I had this significant . . . not an expectation, that's for sure . . . but, yes, this hope. The longer it dragged on, the more I would think, *Yeah, we might get in*. I don't know. I think the odds are strongly against us at this point."

Her call waiting beeps.

"Oh, hold on, just a sec." In a moment Lauren is back, her voice now a different color, full of heat, closer to her normal high energy level.

"That's my friend Susan. She just got her letter from Pemberley. She got rejected."

"She didn't get on the waitlist?"

"Nope. *Rejected*," Lauren repeats. "She's upset but not devastated. Darcy is her first choice. I'm going to get back to her. Compare notes."

"I'll talk to you. And I'm sorry."

"Thanks. Damn. Now I'm thinking about being put on the waitlist. Maybe there is, oh no, that word again, hope." She moans slightly. "This is my worst nightmare. Because it's not over."

We'll See You Soon

One Thursday evening, three weeks before the admissions letters are to be sent out, Katie Miller drives to Hunsford School to attend a coffee for prospective parents. In the words of her husband, it's Katie's last chance to kiss some serious ass.

"I'm not sure what the purpose of the coffee is," Katie says, pulling into the parking lot. "Maybe it's just another part of their weeding-out process. They see the people who show up as *really* serious. Or it could simply be a final opportunity for them to take a closer look at people they're on the fence about. I can't imagine that they need to sell themselves."

After finding a parking space, Katie checks her appearance in her rearview mirror, then strides onto the Hunsford campus as if she owns the place. She swings open the blue door leading into the multipurpose room and encounters a group of about thirty people, nervous and nametagged, most holding Styrofoam coffee cups and paper plates dotted with Pepperidge Farm cookies. As Katie comes into the room, she spots Brianna standing in the far corner engaged in lackluster conversation with a heavily coiffed woman in a pinstriped suit. Brianna seems barely awake as the woman drones on. Katie decides to grab a cup of decaf and head over there, interrupt if need be, and get to work. Halfway across the room, Miranda Gary, president of the Parents' Association, cuts her off.

"So *glad* you could make it," Miranda trills, squeezing Katie's left biceps in greeting.

"Well, I wouldn't miss it," Katie says, which is not party talk but the deepest truth.

"This is a wonderful opportunity to ask any questions about Hunsford that you never had the chance to ask before and to spend some quality time with Brianna. And there will be a short PowerPoint detailing the Hunsford curriculum. That alone is worth it."

That I can do without, Katie thinks.

"You, of course, know Brianna?" Miranda says, her eyes blinking rapidly as if she is in the midst of a college REM experiment.

"We've met. I don't know if she remembers me. She interviews so many parents."

"Come. Let's get reacquainted," Miranda croons, her hand now on Katie's elbow steering her across the room as if she were a blind person.

Before they even approach striking distance, Brianna swivels toward them, eager to disengage from Pinstripe. She extends a bony hand to Katie, who grasps it warmly, firmly, careful not to apply too much pressure or to, God forbid, unknowingly crush her fingers.

"Katie Miller. Not sure you remember—"

"Of course I remember. Your daughter's Alex, right?"

Well, that's all it takes. Mention the kid and the smile is a sunburst.

"I remember *her* very well," Brianna continues. "She had a wonderful visit. So sweet."

"Thanks," Katie says. "We like her."

She laughs, Miranda giggles, then winks at Katie and veers off to intercept a confused-looking latecomer. Brianna smiles, allowing Katie her opening. She doesn't need more than a sliver. She is off and running, diving into an eight-minute conversation, Katie will estimate, that includes the discussion of a wonderful parenting book Katie has just read, which Brianna recommended during their interview, the increased traffic flow in the city, thankfully not a problem for Katie because she's only five minutes away, climaxing with Katie's stating again, for the millionth time, that Hunsford is far and away her first choice. Two other parents, a couple suited in matching charcoal silk, smelling of wealth, appear, and Brianna shifts away from Katie to them, signaling the end of their time together with a subtle finger wave. Bonding-wise, the rest of the evening is uneventful, the PowerPoint providing a rehash of Hunsford's philosophy, but the presentation is so slick and professionally accomplished that it actually amps up her desire for the school even more.

The evening ends on a high note, a moment that makes it all worth it. On behalf of the Hunsford Parents' Association, Miranda thanks the thirty prospective parents for coming to visit Hunsford again, "on a school night," an expression that evokes a larger than deserved laugh. Thank-yous all around and Katie, seeing Brianna again painted into the corner, decides she will not leave without saying a proper good-bye. She makes her way through a cluster of stragglers and smiles at the director of admissions, who smiles back.

"It was so nice talking with you," Katie says.

"Likewise," Brianna says. "We'll see you soon."

Driving home, Katie ponders Brianna's words.

"She said, 'We'll see you soon.' Was that a reaction, a reflex, like something innocuous you say to somebody when they're leaving, or was she giving me a little hint? I don't know. But she knew my name. I can't believe she remembers everybody's name, unless she's letting you in. Or unless she's giving us the boot."

Katie bites her lip. "Three weeks from tomorrow. I think I've hit the wall. I just want to know. Why do they wait so long to send out the letters? They drag it out forever. It's torture. I feel like I can't even go back to my life until I know where my kid is going to school. I'm in limbo."

She drums her fingers on the steering wheel.

"Limbo Woman," she says. "That's who I am. Just *tell* me. Put me out of my misery so I know what I can embrace."

.   .   .

On Friday, March 25, the day the letters arrive, Katie decides to host a party for herself, "Katie's Acceptance Letter Bash," she calls it. The guest list is small and exclusive. She invites only Trina and her close friend Erika, who has a son entering kindergarten in her local public school. Since her mail doesn't usually come until four o'clock at the earliest, Katie calls the party for three-thirty, just to be safe. She considers chasing down the mail carrier the day before and tipping him twenty dollars to guarantee a four o'clock delivery, but he is nowhere to be found.

"You never know when the mail's gonna come," Katie says. "Could be four, could be five. I really don't know. In any case, be prepared to imbibe large amounts of alcohol. Champagne, if the news is good, vodka, if it's not. Either way, I plan to drink heavily."

Trina calls her Friday morning just after eleven. "My mail came," she says. Her voice is flat.

"*Tell* me."

"You were right. I got into all three."

"My God, Trina! That's *great*. I am so happy for you."

"I'm kind of amazed, actually. I honestly didn't think—"

"Trina."

"Okay, okay, I'm sorry . . . Katie, do you really think the Mexican thing helped?"

"*Duh.*"

"I'm not so good at this getting-what-I-asked-for thing. I'm much better at being pissed off and cynical."

"I can't believe Pascal will be among the elite at Meryton. *Score.*"

Trina rubs her forehead. She feels a dull ache pulsing over the bridge of her nose. "Actually, I'm thinking about sending him to St. Mary's."

"You were serious about that? Trina, nobody turns down Meryton."

"I know. I just think St. Mary's might be better for him. Meryton has the great reputation of coddling the kids, taking care of them, all of that. I think Pascal needs more structure and—I can't say this to anyone but you—more discipline. He really does."

"It's such a drive."

"That's the least of it. I'll do it. He's my kid."

"You should sleep on it."

"I know," Trina says. "I have some time. I'm definitely going to sleep on it."

But Katie knows Trina has already made up her mind.

• • •

"Four-fifteen and I'm mail-less," Katie says Friday afternoon, leaning against her kitchen counter. Her friend Erika Nahagian, a dark-haired, husky-voiced beauty wearing a white T-shirt, jeans, and a somber expression, stands propped against the oven. Delayed, Trina has called three times on her cell. In the midst of errands, she and Pascal are tangled in traffic on the east side of town and are not expected for another hour.

"This is exasperating," Erika says. "Mail should arrive by three o'clock at the latest."

"I'm pouring myself a drink," Katie says. "Want one?"

"Yes, please," Erika says. "Is there vodka?"

"Vats," Katie says.

"We're saving the champagne," Erika announces.

Katie pours two fingers of vodka, straight, no ice, no chaser, into two glasses. Erika takes one of the glasses and holds it at eyebrow level.

"To getting in," she says.

"I'll drink to that," Katie says. She plunks her glass against Erika's, takes a long swallow, and smacks her lips.

"Mommy." Alex, dragging a tattered teddy bear by its ear, staggers into the kitchen. She pops her thumb into her mouth.

"What, baby?" Katie says, crouching down to her daughter. "Are you tired?"

Alex nods, rests her head against her mother.

"We got home from my in-laws' at like two in the morning," Katie explains. "She's wasted. Come, let's chill, okay?"

Katie lifts Alex into her arms and carries her from the room. Erika sips her drink, wipes her mouth with the back of her hand.

"This is a phenomenon, in a way," Erika says. "I mean, I live in a neighborhood that's fancy. A lot of wealthy people, well-known people. We all send our kids to public school. Getting into Hunsford or Meryton is a prestige thing, like wearing the right label. Meryton is—"

She waves a hand high above her head, a gesture that implies that Meryton exists in some other dimension.

"I don't think the kids at Meryton are getting a better education. Or if they are, it's certainly not twenty thousand times better."

Another hit of vodka. Erika peers into her glass, tries to conceal her look of amazement that half her drink is gone.

"What I do like about the process, though, is that when you think about it, it's kind of democratic. You go, you interview, you try your best to impress each of the schools, and everybody has a chance, no matter where you live. So even if you don't have a good public school, you do have the opportunity to go private. Being so close with Katie, I feel like I've gone through the whole thing with her. I feel so sorry for her. It's been a roller coaster."

Katie returns to the kitchen, makes a beeline for her drink. "I put Alex down. She may take a short nap."

Katie takes a quick gulp, slides the glass onto the counter. "I heard what you said about your public school. I started there, thought that I could make ours work for Alex. But there were so many things that bothered me. I wanted public school. I went to public school, Miles did, why shouldn't our kids? Well, everything's changed."

"I think you should've called in all your favors. That's the only way to get into some of these schools," Erika says, her point about the process being democratic blurring in an apparent vodka haze.

An hour passes. Alex naps fitfully for fifteen minutes, stumbles out of her bed, gets into a fight over some toy with Nick.

Katie referees, settles them down, comes back, then steps outside to search for the mail truck. Erika deals with her kids, who are restless, bored, and perhaps hungry. Five-thirty approaches. Nobody expected the mail to be this late. At five-forty, a dog barks, a signal, and Katie and Erika, both buzzed, in the living room now, run for the front door. Katie flings it open, shields her eyes with her hand.

"It's here."

"Finally," Erika says, her hand a visor, too.

"Of all days," Katie says.

"I'm dying," says Erika.

"*You're* dying?" Katie laughs, loudly.

A kid screams somewhere in the back.

"Shit," Katie says.

"Mine," says Erika. She heads off. Katie stays cemented to the front walk, her hand shading her forehead. She sways slightly. Waiting.

"Maybe I should go over to him, get the mail myself," she says. "Screw it. I've waited this long. What's two more minutes?"

Erika, kid quieted and banished to the backyard, returns to an empty living room. She hurls herself onto the couch. "My heart is beating. I'm really nervous."

A moment later, Katie comes in holding a small pile of letters, a magazine, and one large envelope.

"Only one big one," she says, brandishing the envelope.

Silence.

"One big one?" Erika says. "From where? From *where?*"

"Evergreen." Katie's voice has flatlined. She speaks as if someone has died. She tosses the Evergreen envelope onto the coffee table. It slaps onto a small stack of *Time*s and *Newsweek*s, bumps into an unopened bottle of Dom Pérignon.

"From Evergreen?" Erika, searching for the right tone, failing, her disappointment leaking out. "Did you get everything?"

"I think so," Katie says, her voice hitting a high note, out of control. She holds each of the remaining four admissions letters, weighing them in the palm of her hand. "Okay. Meryton is no. Hunsford is no. Warwick is no. Bingley is no."

"Are you sure? How do you know for sure?"

"That's what it says." Katie's voice an alien lilt now.

"It says no on the front?"

Katie, all patience, as if explaining to Alex, says, "No. Look." She picks up the large Evergreen envelope, stabs it at Erika as if it's a weapon. "This is the welcome packet. I didn't get in anywhere else."

After a beat, Erika says, "Let's make sure. They might say congratulations."

Katie bobs her head slowly in a kind of yoga motion, then rips open the Hunsford envelope, pulls out the letter, and reads, "I am pleased to offer you a place—"

"YESSSS!" Erika screams.

"In our waiting pool." Katie stares at the letter and says, "Fuck you."

"Aw fuck," Erika says. "Why do they start with 'I am pleased'? That's so unfair. The waiting pool."

Katie doesn't look up from the letter. She reads it once, then again, perhaps trying to will it to transform into different words offering a different conclusion.

"Yep," she says finally, still not looking up. "The. Waiting. Pool."

"Shit," Erika says, then, softly, "Are you sad?"

"I'm . . . disappointed," Katie says. Eyes still fastened on the letter, her fingers clinging to the margins.

"You're not going to open Meryton's?"

"No. Why should I? It's the same thing. All the little ones are the no's." Still holding the Hunsford letter, she reaches over and tears open the letter from Bingley. She reads the letter rapid-fire, refuses to articulate any of the words.

"You have *bumbumbumbumbumbum*. Yeah. Waitlist. Okayyy."

"Well, at least you made the waitlist," Erika says, not daring to look at her.

"Evergreen offered us a space. Warwick? Another little one." Katie doesn't even bother to open that one either. A pause.

"I'm disappointed," Katie says, her voice trembling. This time *disappointed* is clearly code for *devastated*.

"I would be heartbroken," Erika says.

"This is a vodka day," Katie says. "Fuck the champagne." She rips open the remaining two letters, speed-reads through them, and says again, "This is really disappointing."

"Are you going to go to Evergreen?"

"No," Katie says. "I don't think so."

"What are you going to do?"

"I don't know."

She reaches for the Evergreen packet, opens it, and pulls out a contract. She nods, confirms that they have indeed invited Alex to become a member of their incoming kindergarten class, shoves the contract back inside the envelope. "I'm gonna call Miles."

She stands up, teeters for a second, eyes the champagne bottle with some combination of rage and sadness, and leaves the room.

"I don't like the 'I am pleased,'" Erika says. "That's unfair. I got excited for a second."

Erika sighs, sifts through the four letters scattered on the coffee table, remnants of destruction. She picks up one, reads it briefly, puts it back onto the pile. "I know they loved Alex. How can they not love her? How can they not want this family?"

Katie returns, a cordless phone attached to her ear. "It just says waiting list. There are no numbers. It's a wait pool. I don't know if it's random or not."

She picks up the Hunsford letter, looks it over again, then reads it aloud into the phone. "It opens with, 'I am pleased to offer you a place in our waiting pool at Hunsford School.' Isn't that crazy? Anyway, I just wanted to call you and let you know. I'll speak to you. Okay. Bye."

Katie clicks off the phone and tucks herself into the corner of the couch. Her outside hand reveals a freshly poured glass of vodka, this time three fingers on the rocks.

"Oh well," she says.

"You can still try the lottery at my public school," Erika says.

"How am I gonna get in there? It's impossible." Katie reaches down and picks up the Hunsford letter. She reads it through again, nods as if digesting the news for the first time, and throws the letter into the air. It flutters to the floor, three feet from the couch.

"Can you believe this? I'm stunned. I'll tell you what made me think I had a chance at Hunsford."

"They loved Alex," Erika says.

"Actually, it was Evergreen that loved Alex. I can still go to Evergreen. That's the thing. But the reason I thought I had a chance was at that coffee Brianna said to me, 'We'll see you soon.'"

Erika lowers her eyes, sips her drink.

"Okay, here's the deal," Katie says. She pounds back a third of the vodka. Approaching cartoon tipsy, she begins to slur her words. "I know that in the past, a lot of stuff gets shifted around. People get a yes from Hunsford and they end up going somewhere else. And they say no thank you to Hunsford. However . . ."

Another sip. Katie winces, allows the Grey Goose to slide down her throat.

"However," she repeats, the words working their way out in near slow motion, "this year it was so many people's first choice."

"No, but I think they're lying," Erika says. "I do. I think everybody says that every school's their first choice. I know that if I were doing it, I would."

"Yeahhh," Katie says, adrift, not in any condition to argue. She looks out her living room window. She is floating, wondering . . .

"I would say it to every single school," Erika says. She rims her glass with her finger. After several seconds of stone cold silence, she asks, "Are you gonna call them?"

"They're not here. They're on vacation. That's why they do it this way. Everybody's gone."

Katie exhales massively. A sigh of pain, of grief.

"I have heard of people who get in, though," Erika says. "I mean, at the last minute."

She is trying. She never expected this. She came here thinking there would be celebration and champagne.

"I've heard about a lot of people that happened to," Katie says without much conviction. "People who got a call after they'd already sent in their deposit somewhere else. You don't get your deposit back. Well." She pauses. "Let me put my mail away. It's not the best mail."

"What did the Meryton one say?"

"Did I even open it? Oh yeah. I remember. It told me to fuck off."

"No, let's see." Erika rummages through the letters on the coffee table, finds the Meryton letter, and reads, " 'The admissions committee at Meryton' blah blah blah . . . Oh, this is so politically correct. This is *lovely*. 'We think highly of Alex . . .' "

"They think highly of Alex?" Katie says, blasting out a laugh. "They've never met Alex."

"They've never met her? Maybe they just know about her. They've heard about her through the grapevine."

Katie leans forward on the couch. She pats the cushion next to her. Slams her glass on the coffee table. "Okay. Can I be honest with you now?" She holds for a second, perhaps to get her bearings. When she speaks, her words take on a deeper slur. "I am not that surprised. Given the situation. I'm disappointed. I'm mostly annoyed that there is no closure. I was just hoping for closure today. There is no closure."

"What did Miles say?"

"He was like, 'Nothing we didn't expect.' Which is true. He had very low expectations going in. He protected himself. I had high expectations going in."

"Well, for her to say, 'We'll see you soon.' That really threw you off."

"I thought we truly had a connection at that coffee. And our interview went so well. Even then she said, 'Let's look at the positive side.' Maybe that's her spiel. If it is, she ought to change it."

Katie stares off. She blinks once. "I should've protected myself. Our preschool director did tell me that there were already so many sibling spots taken from our school. She said there were only so many more Hunsford could take. And I knew one family who was our competition. She has two major connections there. *Major* connections. I guess I couldn't compete with that. I don't know."

Katie brushes a finger across her nose and faces Erika. "Part of this is ego, too. Trust me. *Trust* me. My ego is bruised."

"Katie, it's not personal."

"Maybe not. But you want to be the one," Katie says, roaring by her, a runaway train. "You want to be the one who got in no matter what connections *they* had. *Good family. We want them. We have to have them.* It's more political than anything. That's what I think."

"I really think you have to know somebody," Erika says.

Silence now as both women sip their drinks. Katie's eyes begin to flutter; she is fighting to keep them open. If Erika were not here, she would curl up on the couch and crash for the night.

"One of Alex's best friends applied," Katie says. "I wonder if she got in."

"Why don't you call her?"

"No. I can't. It's too raw. I can't." Katie closes her eyes. "They're a nice family." And she whispers, "But we're better. Alex is better."

From another room, Alex calls out, "Mommy, I need you."

Katie sighs. "I'm coming, love." She pushes herself up from the couch. "Just hearing her voice now, I don't know, it breaks my heart."

She slowly leaves the room.

"I feel like I'm in a state of mourning," Erika says. "It's like there's been a big loss."

She nods once, as if she's come to a sudden realization, discovered a hidden truth. "She's going to get in off the waitlist. I feel that. Hunsford is going to come back to her. Meryton, no, forget it. But Hunsford, yes, it's going to happen. I suddenly feel it. They're coming back."

Katie returns to the living room, stops at the edge of the couch. "She's so tired, poor thing." She picks up her glass, doesn't drink, uses it instead as a prop, waving it to make a point. "You know, there is always the option of keeping her at Bright Stars for another year. Doing a pre-K year, then applying again next year."

"She'll be so bored."

"Gracie said that, too. She said don't do it."

"Let me ask you this," Erika says. "Is your public school that horrible?"

Katie's eyes flutter. "Let me be completely honest about our public school. Spanish is the first language for over fifty percent of the kids. Over *fifty* percent. Due to the test score factor, No Child Left Behind, all they're doing is focusing on these kids. Why? TO TEACH THEM ENGLISH SO THEY CAN PASS THE FUCKING TEST. My daughter's *reading*. Sorry. She's getting shoved aside. No child left behind? *My* child is being left behind." Katie collapses onto the couch. Lowers her head, speaks into the cushion. "It's just so . . ." And she whispers, *"Annoying."*

"We have to start a movement," Erika says. "I'm serious. We have to take back our public schools. Can you imagine if we all just sent our kids to our local public schools? It can't be just one person. Everybody has to commit to go."

"But it's about the teachers. You might be able to take back the schools but you can't choose the teachers."

Abruptly, Katie stands. She measures herself before she speaks. This is to be her final word on the subject for now. She will not speak about it again until Miles comes home, at which point she will kiss Alex and Nick good night, wrap her hand around the rest of the Grey Goose, polish off the bottle, and fall into a coma-like sleep, awakening at eight the next morning with a hangover headache one tick below a migraine.

"It's just school," she says. "But at the end of the day, I love my kids so much that I want the best for them. Why can't I have it? Why? What did I do? I'm real calm right now. But part of me wants to put my hand through the wall. I know. I got into a school. Not the school I wanted. Didn't get lucky. I have luck in the important things in life. Kids, men, health—knock wood—friends. It's the other bullshit things in life. Want to know why I'm pissed off and shitfaced right now? Because of the irony. That's right. The *irony*. I wasn't even going to go through this process. And then I saw Hunsford and I wanted it. I gave up everything for one year, devoted my entire life to getting us into Hunsford. That became my job. Miles has his job. His job is to bring in the money. My job was to get us into Hunsford. And you know what? I failed. I fucking failed. I'm a failure. Today I got fired from my job."

The ice in her glass clinks as she heads now for the bottle.

CHAPTER NINE

The Second Season

I know it's hard for parents to believe this, but I am on pins and needles waiting to see who is going to accept their spot.

—a private school director of admissions

You Have to Get Over the Names

For many directors of admissions, the most anxiety-producing part of the application process begins the day the letters go out.

"It is hell for an entire month, end of March through the end of April," Dana Optt said. "A lot of stuff moves around. It is an incredibly stressful time. I call it the second season."

Some schools agonize over the diversity children they have accepted. "You never know who is going to come," one head of school said. "This year I took eight kids with full or nearly full scholarship packages. They're exceptional kids and fabulous parents. I don't expect to get all of them. We're far for them, way across town. And we're in a neighborhood that's completely foreign to them. Talk about strangers in a strange land."

"I feel for them, I really do," a director of admissions added.

"I'm in competition for almost all these kids. I don't know what kind of scholarship packages the other schools offered. I do know which schools took them. I have to see what happens, see how many I get. And then I'll go to the waitlist."

Dana Optt, perhaps uniquely, offers herself as a resource, consultant, and facilitator to many of the families she has rejected. "The main thing that happens during the second season is that of the three hundred people I've seen, two hundred and fifty want to talk to me. Sounds crazy, but I talk to as many of them as I can. I try to explain why they didn't get in. I hold their hands. And if I can, I try to place people. My attitude is, why shouldn't I help another school? We all feed off each other. And I want good people to land on their feet. They should be placed. Maybe they didn't think of such and such a school. At least now they can feel like, 'Well, I would've loved to have gotten into Pemberley, but instead I'm in this other school and it's a really good place. I found a home.' The key thing is, you've got to get over the names."

.　.　.

A short time after Lauren's phone call, Craig Pernice escorts his client to the door, returns to his desk, and dials Dana Optt. When he identifies himself to Gail, Dana's assistant, her voice changes direction abruptly, rising from a tone of solemnity into one oozing warmth and welcome. Her hairpin turn surprises Craig. After all, they've only made the waitlist; they're not *in*. He has to admit that talking to Gail makes him feel as if he's won something, a consolation prize at least, and that there just might be hope.

Dana gets on the phone immediately. "I know you didn't get the result you wanted," she says. "I'm really sorry. It was a very tough year for boys. But I want you to know, we love your family, and we *love* Killian. I also want you to know that this is a real waitlist. It truly is. I don't send out a blanket waitlist letter to everyone who applied."

"So it's selective?"

"Very much so. I only take ten boys and ten girls. I can't make any promises but there usually is some movement."

Dana stops now, waits for Craig. She would never cop to it, but it is in some way a test. How he responds to bad news is key. Craig is well-known in town, prominent in his field, someone who is used to winning. Dana has turned him away, denied him something that she knows he wants very much. It is a loss.

Let's see how he handles it.

"I'm disappointed," Craig says. "We love Pemberley. We think it's the perfect place for Killian and for us. But I understand. You have a very tough job. I'm sure there are a lot of wonderful families that you would love to take but you can't because of circumstances. I respect that. I just wanted to call and thank you for putting us on the waitlist. We'll be patient and hold a good thought. If it's meant to be, great."

On the other end of the phone, Dana smiles. Craig's answer is a home run. She doesn't know if he's sincere or if he is a master game player or both. It doesn't matter. In the thirteen years of a child's education from kindergarten through twelfth grade, there are certain to be bumps in the road. Seeing how Craig responded to this first bump validates not only the Pernice family, but Dana's decision to choose them.

"Thank you for understanding. Some people don't," Dana says. "I'll keep you posted."

"I appreciate that. Thanks, Dana."

She hangs up and immediately relives the conversation she

finished fifteen minutes ago with a dad whose daughter she'd waitlisted. While Craig was gracious and humble, this guy was stunned his daughter wasn't accepted. He wanted answers. He wanted to know the breakdown of the waitlist, wanted to know if the list was ranked ("It's not," Dana said), wanted to know the numbers of siblings who were accepted, the boy-girl ratio, early-year versus late- and middle-year acceptances, and he wanted to know his chances. By the end of this conversation, Dana was second-guessing herself, wondering if she had made a mistake. No, she told herself. She loved the kid, loved the mom, but now, thanks to the father, if she were to rank the waitlist, they would slide to the bottom.

• • •

"This is nerve-racking," Lauren Pernice says to a friend over coffee. "First of all, I'm alone. I have not heard of one other family who got waitlisted at Pemberley. I'm like the Chosen One. This woman I know said to me the other day in carpool, 'How did *you* get on the waitlist?' She said it with such contempt and suspicion, as if I paid somebody off or something. She was so resentful. I frankly never expected that reaction. It really threw me off.

"The truth is I am a complete and total wreck. This is absolutely the worst. Much worse than the whole process of filling out the applications, agonizing over the interviews, all of that. It's way more stressful. I don't sleep. I'm not eating. I leap ten feet every time the phone rings. Praying it's Dana. Praying a spot has opened up for Killian. And I'm having all these horrible, terrible thoughts. I know that Dana is waiting to hear who is accepting their spots. There have to be a few people who are not going to come, for whatever reason. I know the minority kids she accepted can't all come to Pemberley. It's so far from where they live. The best of these kids, I'm sure, got in everywhere. Meryton wants them, Darcy wants them; they all want them. So here I am, and I'm ashamed to admit this, rooting against some poor little African-American or Latino boy. Not rooting against *him* exactly. Just hoping he'll choose some other school and give Killian his spot. It's dreadful. I know. I'm a horrible person. I never thought it would be like this."

.   .   .

The news comes to Craig in the form of Lauren's voice mail.

"Guess what? *WE'RE IN!* I just got off the phone with Dana. We've been accepted off the waitlist. Can you believe it? We're in *Pemberley*. Amazing. Kind of otherworldly, actually. Well, that was easy, right? Call me."

.   .   .

When I ask Dana how and why Killian Pernice got in, she flips open the file folder in front of her with the delicate precision of a safecracker.

"The Pernices. They came to the Private School Expo at Darcy, which was very interesting. Before that they were not considering Pemberley. Okay, the parents' interview. Obviously, you look at the two of them, the gene pool looks pretty good. The dad is a prominent guy but very down-to-earth. That speaks volumes to me. Now, this year it was much more competitive for boys. My siblings, faculty, and alumni were predominately boys. It was much easier to find an open spot for a girl. Changes from year to year. As I was putting the class together, I had Killian on and off the initial accept list twenty times. The problem is how many kids are there like him? A million of them apply here. I went for geography. Went for a push from lower-income areas. When one of them turned me down, I knew I could get him off the waitlist. The other thing he did, the dad, when they didn't get in, he made one call. No pushing or screaming. One call. He said, 'If it's meant to be, if we get in off the waitlist, it would be wonderful. But I understand it's difficult. Thank you.' I was thinking, *How are you at handling a situation that you're not happy with and you're high-profile?* Oh, they've got plenty of money. So how he responded to adversity clinched the deal."

Dana shuts the folder, the Pernice case closed. She never mentions Third Guy.

● ● ●

After leaving the news of Killian's acceptance to Pemberley on Craig's voice mail, Lauren Pernice marches into her small office off the kitchen, opens a desk drawer, pulls out the application packet for Wickham School, and dumps it into the wastebasket. She then lets out a huge, involuntary, body-shaking sigh. She feels as if she's opened up an internal release valve and allowed all the pressure to escape.

With purpose, Lauren strides into the kitchen. Using both hands, she swings open the refrigerator and grabs a celebratory Snapple. She swigs mightily, checks the clock on the microwave, and calculates that she has time for two quick phone calls before she has to leave to pick up Killian at preschool. She calls her friend Susan, gushes her news onto her voice mail, then calls another friend and, briefly, humbly, tells of her triumph. Her friend, a mom with a child a year younger than Killian, screams into Lauren's ear. Surprised, embarrassed even by her friend's reaction, Lauren ends the conversation abruptly, saying she has to leave.

She arrives in Killian's classroom thirty minutes later. Incredibly, the news of their getting into Pemberley has spread like wildfire. People Lauren knows casually rush over to her and offer congratulations. The director of the school sprints out of her office and engulfs her in a bear hug, teammates sharing a championship victory. Getting into Pemberley has catapulted Lauren into an instant celebrity.

At dinner the next night, her close friend Wendy says over salad, "People are talking. They heard you got into Pemberley. Everybody wants to know: how did you do it?"

Lauren isn't sure what to say.

"I slept with the director," she says finally.

"Seriously," Wendy says, "how did you get in?"

"You want the truth?"

Wendy nods vigorously. Lauren looks at Craig. His face is stony. He shrugs.

"Connections," Lauren says. "Pure social capital. We knew someone."

Wendy and her husband stare at Lauren. They are mesmerized by her honesty.

"Look, Killian was a good candidate," Lauren says after a sip of wine. "Craig and I had a good interview. I didn't think so at the time, but in retrospect we did. We have means, and Killian did well in his assessment. His performance was essential. If he hadn't done well, we wouldn't have gotten in. I'm sure of that. But the reason this process is so trying is because it's so capricious. The candidates are four and five years old. They don't have résumés and grades and scores and so forth. So who you know plays a large part. It depends on the schools you're applying to as well. I know people who got into Evergreen and Bingley who got waitlisted at Hunsford and Meryton. And then of course you hear about certain preschools that are feeders."

Lauren sips her wine. "People go into this process very naively. They all believe that it's about the kid. We all think our kids are superstars. I'm sure Killian is. But even if he had done just okay on his assessment, we would have gotten in. If you want to get into one of the elite private school kindergartens, it's about money, diversity, and connections. It just *is*. You have to know that going in. Unless you're pretty prominent or rich or diverse yourself, you're going to need some help."

Lauren's pronouncement has somehow left a chill in the air. Sensing the discomfort from Wendy and her husband, Craig catches Lauren's eye. She knows now to change the subject.

"I feel so lucky," Lauren says. "Pemberley is a fabulous school. And it starts right away. There is a parent coffee thing next week for all the incoming kindergarten parents. Hopefully I'll meet some nice people there, people I can relate to. We'll see. Because now I am one of them."

It's Kind of the Least You Can Do

Shea Cohen dabs her eyes with a wad of balled-up Kleenex. The improbable has happened. Liam has gotten into the gifted program at Netherfield off the waitlist. Shea has been crying.

"I never expected this. Not in a million years. It never happens. Well, it happened. Liam's in."

She blows her nose. "The program at Netherfield is so right for him. We went there today, took a really extensive tour, went all through the place. I came out of there heartbroken. It's a public school. The building is so *bleak*. They have no facilities. Their basketball court is a mess, there's no art room, no science lab. I know, I know. You get what you pay for. And Liam isn't really an athlete so he's not giving up anything there. It's just that it was depressing. My heart sank."

She sighs. "But again, you look at what the kids are doing. In first grade they're doing second and third grade stuff. It's so academically challenging. The teacher was excited. The kids were engaged. Liam will thrive there. It's the right thing to do."

Shea's eyes begin to well up. "Yesterday when we first told him, he didn't say much of anything. He seemed fine. Donald and I were a little concerned because his best friend is going to Longbourne. That was part of what made getting in there so cool. Liam and his best friend would both be going. When we told him that he was going to Netherfield and Billy wasn't, he sort of shrugged and said, 'That's okay.'"

She pats her eyes with the clump of tissue. "This morning he was just lying in bed, wasn't really moving. I said, 'Liam, come on, you have to get up for school.' He said, 'Remember yesterday I said that I was okay about going to Netherfield? Well, today, not so okay.' And he started to cry. He said, 'I don't think I'm ever going to see Billy again.' He was really upset. I told him he would see Billy all the time. I promised him he could have as many play dates as he wanted and that we could even work out a schedule where they could hang out on a regular basis. I'll do everything I can to maintain their friendship. The reality, of course, is that you never know."

Shea lobs the Kleenex into a wastebasket. "I had Donald deal with Longbourne. I told him, 'I've carried the ball this whole way, done almost this entire process myself. You're gonna talk to MK and our preschool director. It's kind of the least you can do.' So he did. MK was great. Expressed the appropriate combination of disappointment and understanding.

Left the door open. If Netherfield doesn't work out for whatever reason, there's always a space for Liam. Which is nice to know. Now, if we had said we were bailing for another private school? Don't think it would have gone so well. On the other hand, our preschool director is pissed. *Pissed.* She does not want us to go to Netherfield. She gave Donald a bunch of rhetoric. 'Liam will be a star at Longbourne.' Probably true. But he won't be challenged. I think he'll be bored out of his mind. 'The facilities are nothing like Longbourne's.' True again. Then she went for the jugular. 'He'll be so much more comfortable at Longbourne because he'll go in with his best friend.' Low blow."

A timer dings in the kitchen. Shea stands. She has been baking a batch of cookies for Liam's class. "I think it's all about the yield. In her case, the reverse yield. She gets no points for kids choosing a public school, because even though Netherfield is a gifted school within a school, it still counts as public school. We took a kid out of her private school pool. Points against her. We messed up her record. Kind of sick."

And then Shea allows herself a crooked smile.

"Welcome to New York," she says.

I Just Wanted a Choice

On a Sunday afternoon in early April, fog has socked in the Millers' side of town, threatening to keep it hazy and gray until nightfall. In the kitchen, where Katie and Trina sit at the oval oak table, sweet moist air floats through the open window. They pick at a bowl of fresh strawberries that Katie has placed between them. Outside, children scream. Howls of joy. Miles is in the backyard, giving the women a break, playing God knows what with Alex, Pascal, and Nicky.

Katie sits at the edge of her chair, on edge being her perpetual state for two weeks now. She has slept only in spurts since the Hunsford waitlist letter arrived and has lost her appetite. She looks thoughtfully at a strawberry before resting it on the table in front of her.

"You almost ate that," Trina says. "That would've been a breakthrough."

Katie shrugs, rolls the strawberry around beneath her palm. "I've never heard of anyone turning down Meryton," she says.

"You're right. It's not done," Trina says.

"But you're gonna do it."

"I am."

"You're sure?"

"I'm not. I'm probably crazy."

A kid shrieks. The women stiffen, poised to bolt from their chairs and charge outside. The shriek dissolves into a laugh.

"That was Pascal," Trina says. Her expression shifts. Her mocha complexion deepens. Seriousness darkens her skin tone, as if she is accumulating a tan. "The biggest plus for Meryton is that I won't have to go through this stupid process again. St. Mary's stops at sixth grade."

"Have you sent in the deposit?"

"Yep. We're going. It's weird. St. Mary's is so off the map. Nobody turns down Meryton and nobody goes to St. Mary's. But I really think it'll be better for Pascal. It's the right fit. At least I think so. What do you think?"

Katie laughs. "Don't ask me."

Then in one fluid, violent move, Katie snatches the strawberry and stuffs it into her mouth. "I like Evergreen, you know?" she says, chewing. "I've always liked the school. Otherwise I would not have *applied* to the school."

She slows her speech down to a crawl, measuring each syllable.

"It wasn't my first choice. We know that. I am still reeling from the disappointment of not getting in. *Still* reeling. I just wish I had a choice. I wish I got into two schools. That's all I wanted. Two schools."

Trina touches Katie's arm. Katie sits up straight as a pole. The move knocks Trina's fingers off of her arm.

"Having said that, I want to tell you that I have been doing some research into Evergreen."

Trina brightens. This is news. "You have?"

"Yes. And the research has led to intensive soul-searching."

"Soul-searching can be a big plus."

"I'm liking the school more and more."

"Score," says Trina, a smile flashing.

"I spoke to a mom I know at Evergreen. She shared something with me that was really helpful. She feels that Evergreen is what she wishes public schools were like. This city and this process are screwed up in terms of the money and the glitz and the connections and all of that. Evergreen is a pretty low-key place. There is an element of money there, sure, but it's less so than at a lot of other schools. The school certainly doesn't flaunt it."

"It's not showy," agrees Trina.

"Correct. They're kind of saying that growing up in this culture is weird enough. Let's take some of the weird out and be as down-to-earth as we can. Not so easy. But it's a conscious try."

"I'm liking this, too."

"You're already spoken for. You're going to the Catholic school across town."

"Can't wait."

"The other part of the equation is that this mom is such an

enormous fan of the school that it was sort of contagious talking to her. She talks about Evergreen as if there is no other place like it on earth and that it's a privilege to send your kids there. She's the poster mom for the school."

"A lot of people love that school. I hear that a lot."

"It was really good talking to her. I feel so much better. Almost as if a weight has been lifted. I'm starting to *lean*, you know?"

Trina nods. "You're not drinking the Kool-Aid yet but you could be soon."

"A lovely image, but, yes, okay, I could be soon. Like three days. If Hunsford doesn't take us off the waitlist by Wednesday, I think I'll be able to embrace Evergreen. I'll have to."

"You're going to wait until then? You're not going to mail them a check tomorrow?"

"I'm holding on to one last stitch of hope. If I don't hear anything from Hunsford by Wednesday morning before eleven, then I'm driving a check over to Evergreen." Katie pauses. Pulls the strawberries toward her. She stares into the bowl like a fruit inspector. "I was hoping to hear something from Gracie, but I haven't heard a thing. I'm going to call her again tomorrow. Just kind of hoping she's heard from Brianna."

"Did you have anybody call on your behalf?"

"Five people," Katie says, nudging the bowl aside. "Five people called Brianna. Don't know if they're heavy hitters or what but five people spoke for us. The other thing is I don't know where we are on the waitlist. I should say Alex, right? I don't know where Alex is on the waitlist."

"I feel like the end to the pain and suffering is near," Trina says.

"You know what it is? I'm cool with Evergreen during the

day. At night, as soon as my head hits the pillow, my mind starts going into high gear and I come up with all these things about Evergreen that bother me."

"Thank God Alex is going to school during the day," Trina says.

Katie sighs. "I can't wait for this to be over. For a final decision. I want to embrace *something*. This is killing me."

"It's killing me, too, believe me."

Ignoring her, her shoulders sagging, Katie mutters, "I'm not sleeping. The anxiety is keeping me up. My days are a blur. I'm getting less than two hours a night. I'm a seven-hour-a-night sleeper, minimum. I need my rest. I've gotten sick. My resistance is in the toilet."

"All over a school," Trina says.

"It just bugs me," Katie says. "Why did she have to say, 'We'll see you soon'? If she knew we were going to be first or second on the waitlist, fine, great, but you can't let things like that slip out of your mouth. Maybe she ends every interview that way. But it gave us false hope."

"I know," says Trina.

Katie puffs out her cheeks, then allows a thin line of air to slowly escape. "So, okay, if I don't hear anything from Hunsford, I write the deposit check and bring it over to Evergreen. Has to be in by noon, Wednesday."

"How much are they hitting you up for?"

"Didn't I tell you? Forty-five hundred dollars."

Trina almost blurts, "Chalk one up for parochial schools," her deposit being less than two grand, but she holds her tongue and says only, "That's a lot of money."

"Forty-five fifty to be exact," Katie says. "And you know what? If I got a call at 12:01 from Hunsford, I'd eat it."

. . .

On Wednesday morning at 11:45, after a night of virtually no sleep despite swallowing an Ambien at midnight, Katie Miller climbs behind the wheel of her SUV and heads over to Evergreen School, even in traffic just a seven-minute drive. Previously that morning, she'd busied herself with a flurry of household activity: folding laundry, emptying the dishwasher, vacuuming, rearranging the contents of the fridge. Her lack of sleep and poor appetite, combined with her feelings of disappointment, frustration, failure, and loss, have left her emotionally and physically battered. Katie is a woman of high energy and focus, but since receiving the Hunsford letter she has been moving through her life as if trudging through a foot of mud. She is used to getting what she wants, especially when she works hard. She is a person who creates goals and meets them.

But this process has blindsided her. She lies awake at night trying to pinpoint where she went wrong. She probably should have pulled out all the stops before, she thinks. She should have had her contacts at Hunsford write letters to Brianna *before* her interview. She should have been cooler about Alex's visit. Maybe Alex torpedoed her school visit because she was nervous, sensing her mother's anxiety.

And maybe it has nothing to do with her or Alex, and maybe none of it matters. Maybe Evergreen is and has always been their school. And still, Wednesday morning, as she opens her checkbook and prepares to write a check to the Evergreen School for more than four thousand dollars, she stares at the phone, praying that it will ring, and that Brianna is on the line, offering her a spot off the waitlist.

. . .

Wednesday afternoon, Katie navigates her cart over the polished tongue-and-groove floors of the high-end health food store. The ceilings are wood-beamed the color of whole wheat, the aisles crammed with herbal remedies, skin care products derived from goat's milk, and bins of granola, oats, and dozens of varieties of dry and shucked beans. The air hangs heavy with the smell of peach incense.

Katie's cell rings. She fumbles in her purse. Flips it open. Trina.

"How did it go?"

"I'm bummed."

"Oh," Trina says. "Did you bring the check over?"

"Yeah, yeah, yeah," Katie chants in a monotone. "Waited till the last second. Got it in right under the wire."

"I bet they loved that."

"Actually, Connie couldn't have been nicer. She called me yesterday to see if we were coming and I said, 'We're coming with bells on.' I was all enthusiasm. I didn't want her to hear the disappointment in my voice."

Katie parks her cart against a barrel of pinto beans, just missing a woman in a tie-dyed dress comparing two different types of mustard.

"There's been a sort of new development," Katie says, reflexively cupping her hand over the phone.

"What?" Trina's eagerness attached to the word *new* is nearly a shout through the phone.

"Alex's friend, that girl who got into Hunsford *and* Evergreen *and* Bingley?"

"The little princess. Yeah?"

"They chose Evergreen."

A beat. Static through the cell.

"So that's an ouch, right?" Trina says, trying to disguise the hurt that even she feels.

"Major ouch. Why didn't Hunsford replace her with Alex? Are we that far down the waitlist?"

"I don't know."

Katie rubs her forehead. Her head is rumbling. "They're not taking me in the first round, okay. But now I know there's an opening and we're not getting the call off the waitlist? Opening for a girl, too. I'm like shit, fuck, damn, ass."

The mustard lady looks up, cradles both jars, quickly moves away.

"I think you forgot a couple," Trina says.

"I'd rather not let loose. I'm in Whole Foods."

"Alex will have a friend," Trina says. "Look at it that way."

"Yeah, yeah, yeah," says Katie.

"Oh, Katie."

"I'm not *excited*. I want to be at a school that I'm really excited about. This is so much money to pay for seven years of feeling fine, whatever."

"Katie," Trina says, "you have to let go. You have to try to get excited."

"I know," Katie says. "I know I do." Her voice is soft and filled with sadness. "I'm just hoping something gives. That's all."

A stabbing pain arrives above her eyes like a blow to the head. Katie closes her eyes, rubs her forehead in a circle.

"That girl getting off the waitlist," she says, eyes slammed shut. "Why couldn't that have been me? Why do I have such bad luck with this?"

"Maybe it's not bad luck," Trina says. "Maybe this is where Alex is supposed to be."

"I keep telling myself that. I do. The problem is I care too much. When you don't care about something, that's when you get it. I have to figure out a way not to care anymore."

"It's going to be fine," Trina says, exhausted, trying to find a different remedy for the same pain.

"Maybe I just do need to give up hope," Katie says.

"Good. Try that tactic."

"But every time I give up hope I start to get really nauseous."

"Why don't you get out of town? Go skiing. Go to the beach. Go to New York."

Katie opens one eye. She suddenly feels dizzy and weak-kneed. She looks at the floor. She could easily curl up in a fetal position right here, right between the barrel of beans and a bin of oats.

"You've had worse ideas," Katie mutters.

"I have to go," Trina says. "Pascal will be outside karate class waiting for me. You don't want to piss off a five-year-old yellow belt."

"Go," Katie says.

"Call me later. We'll continue this."

"You must hate me. All I do is obsess and bitch and moan."

"You don't moan."

Katie puffs out a small laugh, flips her phone shut, and stuffs it into her purse, which is snuggled against a half gallon of low-fat organic milk and a tub of Greek yogurt, the only two items she has managed to cross off her list, the only two she has had the strength to lift into her cart.

Teacups and Crispies

I tell parents all the time. Don't look too far into the future. Today's messed-up, crazy preschooler is tomorrow's Bill Gates. And today's brilliant, adorable four-year-old is tomorrow's crackhead.

—*an educational consultant*

I Feel Bad Enough as It Is

The letters are written and signed, the envelopes sealed and mailed. The candidates have been chosen. What's done is done.

"When I'm out to dinner with my husband or friends, or I'm in the grocery store, I constantly run into people, either prospective parents or parents I didn't admit. It puts me in such a position," said Brianna, director of admissions at Hunsford. "You have to say hello. It's usually the ones you didn't admit who come over and interrupt your dinner. That doesn't sit well with me. What am I supposed to say? I've *declined* them. There is nothing I can do. I declined them for a reason. If they stopped to think about that for a minute, maybe they wouldn't come over. What do they want to happen? What is coming over going to do? Do they want another opportunity for me to bond with them? It's tough. I already feel bad enough as it is."

Approaching the director of admissions who has turned you down while she's out to dinner is the last-gasp measure of desperate people. Savvy prospective parents, such as Lauren and Craig Pernice, realize that strong candidates for kindergarten are ones with representatives—agents, as it were. In the case of kindergarten admissions, the most effective agents are board members. Or so people think. An example:

A mom told an educational consultant that she was applying to only one school.

"Don't you think that's risky?" the consultant asked.

"No. Because we know we're in."

"That's great," the consultant said. "How do you know you're in?"

"Our neighbor's on the board. He promised that he'd get us in."

They didn't get in. After the family received their rejection letter, the consultant asked the admissions director of that school to define the power board members wielded in the admissions process.

"We knew what that woman was saying. We heard that she was spreading the word that a board member would get her in. That does not happen. There's no way I would take her. She really pissed us off."

Still, prospective parents seek agents in high places. DJ, head of a private school, said, "It's gotten so insane, the stakes seem higher every year. Last year, a lovely family, kind of new to the city, didn't understand the reality. The child was not accepted because he was too young, didn't make the cutoff date. The grandfather, who is a retired CEO, wrote me a letter pretty much begging me to take the child. CC'd George W. Bush. Shall we chew on that for a second? If you're copying the president of the United States over kindergarten admissions, what does that tell you about the stakes?"

Señora Evergreen

After Katie Miller returned from shopping at Whole Foods that day in April, she called Miles and told him that she was fried. She needed some serious R&R. She suggested they go skiing, not something she was desperate to do; it was just the first thing that came to mind. She wanted a change of scenery. She wanted to let the kids run around in the snow while she crashed in the lodge. She needed a break from the city and from her life. Surprisingly, Miles the workaholic agreed. Sliding directly into madwoman overdrive, Katie got everything together in a day. The Millers hit the slopes first thing Saturday morning.

It was heaven. The sky was deep blue and crystal clear, not a cloud. The air was brisk and, it being so late in the season, the slopes were deserted. The kids loved the change of scenery. They had snowball fights and built a snowman. Miles and Nick constructed an elaborate snow fort while pretending to be on some guys' campout thing.

Alex and Katie enjoyed plenty of girl time. Alex had been up on skis before but she'd always been a little hesitant. This time she was confident and ultra-cool. They attacked the baby slope as if they were training for the Junior Olympics. Of course they fell constantly. Each time, they rolled over each other in the snow, laughing hysterically. At night they built a fire, brought in food, and watched DVDs, snuggled together in one bed. They were away for four glorious days.

While they were gone, something changed. Katie could feel a shift. It began as soon as they checked in and it became stronger and stronger as the days went on. The shift felt permanent; Katie could feel it sticking to her as they drove home.

The shift had to do with coming to grips with priorities. Identifying them, owning them, understanding what is truly important in life.

"You always hear people say, 'Life is about family, friends, and health. Everything else is in second place.' I know that," Katie said. "I just forgot about it until we went away. I found this other level with my family. They are my life; they are what I live for. They know it. We all know it. We don't spend time announcing it. They just know it.

"I now truly believe that where Alex goes to kindergarten is not the biggest deal in life. When I project thirteen years into the future, can I see Alex going from Evergreen to Princeton? Maybe. Maybe not. I don't know. No one knows. But now I don't think it matters one iota. If Alex doesn't go to Princeton or some other elite college, does that mean she's not going to make it in life? Is she doomed to be a failure? I seriously doubt it.

"So much of this process was about me. *I* got rejected by the school of *my* choice. She didn't. They don't know her. They met her for forty-five minutes. Maybe it was a lousy forty-five minutes. Who knows?"

In the end, Alex did get into private school. She did get chosen. "Some people didn't get in anywhere," Katie acknowledged. "And the more I think about Evergreen, the more I like it. In fact, if I allow myself, I start to think that maybe Evergreen is the right match for our family. Maybe it was meant to be for Alex, Nick, Miles, who's completely fine with it, and for me. Yes, for me. Maybe it will be the right match for me."

Katie is trying. The day after she got back from vacation she called Connie and told her how happy she was to be a part of the Evergreen community. She told her that she wanted to be involved in any way she could. In fact, she offered to teach Spanish in their after-school program, a couple days a week. Connie loved the idea. She said she'd run it by Edgar, but she didn't see any reason why he wouldn't go for it.

So Katie has begun to embrace the school. "That's the way it has to be," she said. "After all, Alex will be spending more waking hours there than at home. You bet I'm going to be involved. Call me Señora Evergreen."

Now What?

How do you get in?

With admissions directors either unable or unwilling to answer the question, it's no wonder that parents feel helpless and frustrated. They want to know what to *do*. Even if getting in, as some parents believe, means donating a certain amount of money or being connected to the right people, what is that amount and who are those people? Maybe we can raise the money. Maybe we know somebody.

The desperation to get in is fueled by what lurks on the flip side: *not* getting in. The zeitgeist has spoken. Not getting into the "right" kindergarten means the end of the road. You are washed up at five years old. Banished to public school. Kiss the Ivy League good-bye. Say hello to State University.

It is becoming increasingly tempting to buy into this argument. Each year, college admissions offices are flooded with a record number of applications. High school seniors routinely apply to at least a dozen colleges; many apply to as many as *twenty*. Colleges that previously would have been considered safety schools are now only fifty-fifty possibilities.

Our culture has changed. Our children no longer strive for prestigious professions because there no longer are any. Doctors have become "providers," lawyers are a dime a dozen and constantly fight the sleaze factor, the technology revolution has been shipped overseas, accountants are being replaced by Quicken and QuickBooks, and writers? Please. Kids and their parents have adjusted. Prestige is defined now by where you go to college. And in order to get into certain elite schools, it certainly can matter where you go to kindergarten.

But if the admissions process from exclusive kindergarten through elite college resembles a speeding train, as the head of one private school describes, what happens when our children decide to get off?

A striking report in the *New York Times*, headlined "Many Women at Elite Colleges Set Career Path to Motherhood" (September 20, 2005), reveals that "many women at the nation's most elite colleges say they have already decided that they will put aside their careers in favor of raising children." Based on interviews with nearly two hundred Ivy League students, the article reports that "about 60% of the women surveyed would opt for motherhood ahead of a full-time career," with many saying "they will happily play a traditional female role, with motherhood their main commitment." Without question, motherhood ranks among the most challenging, rewarding, and revered careers, but attaining world-class-mother status does not in any way require an Ivy League education.

Which then begs the question: does attending a premier college assure success and happiness?

The answer, of course, is no. Much has been written lately about the migration of graduating seniors from the Ivy League and other name colleges who have taken up residence in their old rooms in the family house. After going through private school since kindergarten, these highly educated young adults discover that without the pressure of classes, homework, and exams, they are now at a loss as to what to do with themselves. One author has called this phenomenon the Boomerang Effect.

A Columbia graduate who sells handmade jewelry in a small high-end boutique spoke about her journey from private school kindergarten to the Ivy League.

"My parents pushed me all the way," she said. "I went to private school and Columbia for them. Now I'm doing what I want to do."

It's easy to imagine her parents torturing themselves over what has become the $500,000 question: "*Was it worth it?* Did we get what we paid for? My daughter is a retail clerk, selling beads for a living. She could've gone to public school and community college and ended up in exactly the same place for $10,000 *total.*"

An educational consultant assessed the value of being admitted to an elite college even more bluntly.

"Just getting in means nothing," she said. "The scary part is that parents are only focusing on how much money their kids are going to make, or what they need to attain a certain status, because they see it's a dog-eat-dog world they're sending their kids into. I guess that's what it's about. They're certainly not thinking of what will make their child happy. That's what they should be doing."

Another educational consultant said, "Getting into an Ivy

League college does not come with a guarantee that your child is going to be a successful human being. He gets into Harvard . . . great. And then what? He's going to come home. They do. And since you've enabled your child every step of the way, he doesn't realize that he now has to make a living, he has to make a life. We are creating this whole group of children who feel *entitled* but don't have a clue about how to accomplish anything. There is a huge difference between feeling entitled and having self-esteem. Self-esteem comes from accomplishing something on your own. To me, that is the key thing. It's way more important to know that your child is happy and feels successful and feels like a viable human being who has an effect on the world. More important than anything else."

The example of the Columbia grad selling jewelry because it's what she really wants to do is becoming more prevalent. Our society is filled with Ivy League graduates, products of private school, who are retail clerks, struggling musicians, starving artists, part-time housepainters, occasional construction workers, and freelance SAT tutors. There is nothing wrong with graduating from college and spending time, sometimes years, finding one's way. In fact, it's common. But that's not what we expected of this group, our preselected elite. These are our best and brightest, the "leaders of tomorrow," as the head of a prestigious Manhattan private school informed the incoming *kindergarten* class. From the moment they entered kindergarten and their parents forked over their first $20,000-plus tuition payment (guaranteed to increase by a minimum of five percent a year for the next twelve years), these "leaders" were groomed by both the private school culture and their parents to achieve. No, to *excel*.

They did not disappoint. They mortgaged large chunks of

their childhoods to become classically trained youth orchestra members, superior club team athletes, and precocious young scientists. They spent their summers taking college courses on Ivy League campuses or in Europe at Oxford or the Sorbonne, or painting bridges and distributing humanitarian aid in third world countries. In the margins of their days, obliterating any leisure time, they wrote prizewinning plays, acted, danced, and sang in professional companies, and interned with renowned scientists or U.S. senators. When they applied to a menu of elite colleges from their equally elite private schools, their applications boasted not only a lofty GPA and staggeringly high SAT scores, but also a portfolio of accomplishments that would surpass professionals who spent a decade in the same pursuit.

The downside to this achieving is what makes some of them return to their rooms. They were so preoccupied padding their résumés for college that they forgot how to dream, how to play, how to *be*. They are products of a system that has molded them into the sum of their test scores, grades, and extracurricular activities. They have succeeded spectacularly; they have been accepted into the college of their dreams, or of their parents' dreams, and now they have discovered that they have no dreams left and no particular place to go. And in more and more cases, kids who have been pushed to achieve by their desperate, aggressive, yet well-meaning parents find themselves emotionally battered by sophomore year.

"Most parents say they want to do what's best for their child," said DJ, the head of a private school. "But in doing what they think is best, they are in fact doing some shortsighted things, which may make their children successful students in the very narrow sense, but really lousy people long-term. There are studies of the top graduates of high schools that show that these kids are crashing and burning in college. The admissions director at Harvard wrote an article that appeared in *Independent School* magazine in which he said that the nicknames for these kids are 'Teacups' and 'Crispies' because they're fragile and burned out.

"It's getting out of control," DJ continued. "The parents have to slow down. They have to try to grasp the big perspective of a lifetime of learning and growing. They are getting so preoccupied with a kindergarten spot. There are lots of other things that are important. Look at your kid. Consider that you've got a whole universe, a life, a four-year-old life, that is going to be around for many years. Don't let your own anxieties color this experience. We think that so much is riding on this. We don't have the perspective yet to see that we're going over the top.

"Also there has been a cultural shift. Parents today are way more involved in their kids' lives than we ever were. Parents organize and orchestrate childhood. As a result, childhood has changed drastically. It's becoming more adult. More professional. I think it's harmful for children. What's interesting is when you look at the lives of really successful people, when you look at where they went to school and how well they did, you often see a story of mediocre grades at a less than elite school. Jack Welch went to UMass, Bill Gates and Steve Jobs both dropped out of college. The list goes on and on. My guess is that as kids these people were not overmanaged, overprogrammed, or overpackaged. They're real people, people who tried things, followed their passions, created dreams, and weren't driven by grades. They have skills that often aren't measured in schools. There is a whole emotional quotient that schools don't measure in a real way. And we should. What's happened is that success is too narrowly defined, mostly by parents. A child's next step for success has become the path to ten elite universities. That's just wrong."

. . .

Perhaps getting into a prestigious private school kindergarten did help our children get into an elite college.

Now what?

Some will graduate and continue to achieve, evolving into who they were groomed to be, our wisest, wealthiest, and most prominent citizens, our adult elite.

Others, anointed at five, are burned out at nineteen.

Or depressed and medicated.

Or lost.

Casualties of what began as the kindergarten wars.

Acknowledgments

The Kindergarten Wars exists because of immeasurable acts of kindness from many parents, educators, admissions directors, and school heads who agreed to speak to me only if I promised them anonymity. While I cannot mention your names, please know that I am deeply grateful to all of you. Without your participation I could not have written this book.

Thanks to Wendy Felson, Lois Baskin, Naomi Press, Mel Foster, Josh and Stephanie Wilson, Randy Feldman, Nancy Lieberman, Sara Fisher, Robin Aranoff, Betsy Brown Braun, Lana Ayeroff Brody, Victoria Goldman, Amanda Uhry, Emily Glickman, Diane Golden, Hugh Gottfried, Gary Yale, Leah Bishop, Elizabeth Yale, Pastor Sweetie Williams, and Manasa Tangalin for generously sharing your time and knowledge, and in many cases introducing me to people who would become integral to the book.

Amy Einhorn is the best editor alive. Amy, your insight, intelligence, persistence, and patience made my book better. The fact that you went into labor while writing my editorial letter *and* completing your daughter's last kindergarten application made this book a true labor of love. A thousand thank-yous. Thanks also to Caryn Karmatz Rudy for filling in with such grace and ease, Jamie Raab, Emily Griffin, Roland Ottewell, Nicola Goode, and special thanks to Wendy Sherman.

David Ritz, again and again, thank you. Many thanks to Shirley and Jim Eisenstock, Madeline and Phil Schwarzman, Susan Pomerantz and George Weinberger, Susan Baskin and Richard Gerwitz, Edwin Greenberg and Elaine Gordon, Randy Turtle, Katie O'Laughlin and everyone at Village Books, and The Cousins—Lini, Lorraine, Dee Dee, Alan, Chris, and Loretta and Brian—who will all be guiding Ben and Nathan into the kindergarten battle sooner than you know it.

During the writing of *The Kindergarten Wars*, my son went through the process of applying to college. I'm not sure which process is more harrowing, applying to kindergarten or college, but somehow our family has survived. Jonah and Kiva, you are both extraordinary. Thank you for putting life in perspective and keeping me sane.

Bobbie, you are my best friend and toughest critic. Simply put, if something passes the Bobbie Test, I know it's good. For more years than I care to count, I've been taking the test and, for the most part, passing. Thank you.

A final note to the moms I followed. In some way, your quests for a coveted kindergarten spot became my quest, and your triumphs, losses, anxieties, and pain became mine as well. In the end, I have painted a picture that is unflinchingly honest and not always flattering. I am deeply thankful to all of you for allowing me to expose your humanity in what was often an inhumane process.